HIDDEN
CORK

MICHAEL LENIHAN

HIDDEN CORK

CHARMERS, CHANCERS AND CUTE HOORS

MERCIER PRESS

IRISH PUBLISHER – IRISH STORY

MERCIER PRESS

Cork

www.mercierpress.ie

Trade enquiries to CMD BookSource,
55a Spruce Avenue, Stillorgan Industrial Park,
Blackrock, County Dublin

First published as a hardback in 2009.
This edition published in 2010.

© Michael Lenihan, 2009

ISBN: 978 1 85635 686 2

10 9 8 7 6 5 4 3 2

A CIP record for this title is available from the British Library

Printed and bound in the EU.

Contents

To my wife Josephine,
my son Andrew,
my daughter Catherine
and grandson Culann

Foreword

Cork, like everywhere else, has a rich and varied history (though Cork's, of course, as any native will tell you, is richer and more varied than most!). Historians set out to describe, explain and analyse the city's past in context, forging long narratives, drawing out links, identifying patterns and probing the dynamics of Cork's political, social, economic and cultural life over the centuries. This is not Michael Lenihan's purpose. He is an avid collector of documents and artefacts relating to Cork's history and with a keen eye and Corkonian's feel for his native place he has delved into his wonderful collection and served us up a cornucopia of Leeside characters, events and places which brings the city's past to life.

This Cork miscellany, in the fine tradition of the late Seán Beecher, shines light into both familiar and unfamiliar corners of the city's history, illuminating – through sketches of weird and wonderful characters, travellers' descriptions, beautiful illustrations, potted histories of buildings and landmarks and succinct accounts of bizarre and fascinating events and episodes – multiple aspects of 'hidden', historical Cork. We descend joyfully in a hot air balloon onto the city's trams, visiting – in no particular order and amongst much more – factories, graveyards, asylums, prisons, hospitals, churches and dispensaries, before observing some bull baiting, starling battles, faction fights and slave escapes in the company of quack doctors, bibliophile bishops, striking workers, bards, beggars and arctic explorers, all lit up by gas lamps and burning buildings.

Michael has a peerless collection of rare illustrations and photographs of historical Cork, a number of which are published here for the first time and are alone worth the cover price.

Informative and entertaining in equal measure, *Hidden Cork* gives the lie to the notion that history can ever be boring. Like all good popular histories, it should encourage some readers, their interest aroused or curiosity tickled by the portrayal of a particular character or event, to delve deeper into aspects of our rich past.

DR DÓNAL Ó DRISCEOIL
Department of History
University College Cork

Quack Doctor in Cork

Baron Spolasco was a notorious quack doctor during the early 1800s. He made spurious claims of successful cures for practically every known disease and affliction at that time. The baron printed leaflets selling his own medical potions such as 'balm of Spolasco' and his famous 'Antiphroditic' cure-all, which apparently never failed. His other infallible cures, 'the life preservers', he claimed, were used in boarding schools, factories, coal and lead mines, and always had the effect of keeping everyone that took them hale and hearty.

During 1837, the bold baron was peddling his wares in Limerick. After his farewell address to the people of Limerick, he proudly announced that he would travel to Cork to afford to sufferers there the benefit of his cures in the most unyielding cases, although other practitioners had pronounced them 'incurable'. This was followed by a series of advertisements in the *Cork Standard*, outlining a list of local cures followed by the sale of 2,000 boxes of his 'vegetable patent pills'. An advertisement in the *Cork Standard* on 4 December 1837 stated:

> I, George Daly, Plasterer North Mall, do certify that Baron Spolasco cured me effectually of a diseased arm (the limb was swelled to an enormous extent), and that I was altogether unable to use a knife and fork and was thus afflicted for three years.

Further miraculous cures were pronounced, such as the case Spolasco recorded in his book, *The Narrative of the Wreck of the Killarney*:

> Mrs Horrigan, wife of a farmer at the Mile-House, Blarney Lane near this city, perfectly cured of cancerous sores upon her nose and face, which for seven years had disfigured her. This person was cured without an operation, and no mark left!

Cornelius Smith of Hammond's Marsh was cured of paralysis of the arm from which he suffered for several years. He was so fully cured that he could return to gainful employment thanks to the baron's medical expertise. The baron successfully treated numerous people, including two patients who were blind for twenty years and could now see thanks to his wonderful treatments. He found it necessary to charge the princely sum of five shillings to a poor person for his advice, but the wealthy would have to pay the usual fee of one guinea – no doubt, a nice little earner at the time. His consulting rooms were at No. 4 King Street (currently MacCurtain Street).

Possibly because he was afraid he would be exposed as a fraud, he eventually decided to leave Cork. The baron said, 'he had received an urgent call from the agent of a person of high personage with regard to a difficult surgical case'. He left Cork with his son Robert and they departed on the paddle steamer the SS *Killarney*. Following the sinking of the *Killarney* and the loss of his son, his next port of call was Glamorgan in Wales. There he had a special medallion struck in his honour. This unofficial advertising token proclaimed that the baron had 5,000 recent astounding cures to his credit.

It is recorded that he treated Susannah Thomas at Bridgend Glamorgan for severe stomach pain. Upon examination, he informed her that he knew by her eyes that she was extremely ill but that he could cure her. He prescribed two pills which he handed to the patient and charged 22s 6d for his services. Susannah's condition grew worse and the baron prescribed a wine-glass full of brandy mixed with a glass of wine stating, 'That will rouse her.' But this concoction did her constitution no good, so the baron revisited the patient. He then administered two spoons of castor oil followed by an ounce of turpentine. Within fifteen minutes, Susannah was dead. The autopsy revealed that she had a duodenal ulcer.

A coroner's court brought in a verdict of manslaughter as the medicine found in the deceased was 'highly injurious'. It also emerged that the baron had treated twelve other patients in Bridgend with the same pills. A warrant was issued for the baron's arrest and he subsequently appeared before the magistrates, and was committed to Cardiff jail to await trial at the next quarter sessions. He wrote to the newspapers saying that it was all 'a foul conspiracy got up against him'.

Following his release from prison, after a successful appeal, he decided to head for America where he was unknown, as it would provide him with rich pickings. He departed for the United States where he frequently appeared in a carriage drawn by four fine horses, hired to cause a sensation. Because of his showmanship and great impudence, he continued to fool many people and made a great deal of money while in America.

Little is recorded about the baron's subsequent life, but he eventually died penniless in New York in December 1858. *The Gentleman's Magazine* of the time records, 'the death recently of the quack, Doctor Baron Spolasco well known in South Wales and Gloucestershire'.

The Sinking of SS *Killarney*

The steamer *Killarney*, heading for Bristol, set sail on the morning of Friday 19 January, 1838, from Penrose Quay at about 9.30 a.m. Captain Bailey was in charge and it had a large cargo of pigs on board. Having left the harbour the weather deteriorated, with heavy falls of snow, and the captain decided to head back to Cobh. The vessel remained at anchor for a time before the captain decided to head to sea once again. It was now dark and the weather soon grew even worse.

At about two o'clock in the morning, the vessel heaved terribly with one passenger shouting 'the vessel is filling, we shall all be lost'. Everything was thrown about and broken on the ship. Carpet-bags, glasses, candlesticks, etc., were strewn everywhere and one hundred and fifty pigs were washed overboard. Because of the heavy mist, no one knew where they were. The engine stopped and the steamer listed. Water poured through a hole in the stern, filling the engine room, and several passengers were washed overboard.

The captain did everything he could to return to Cork Harbour, but the sails were shattered to pieces by the storm and the engine boilers were out of action because of the water. The pumps were the only things keeping the *Killarney* afloat and, when she struck a rock in Rennie Bay, she broke up. The mast, funnel and rigging gave way with a thunderous roar as they bent and cracked, and within an hour no trace of the wreck was visible. A number of passengers made it to a nearby rock with the night approaching, and spent the night clinging onto the rock. Sadly not all survived the cold and dark to see the morning.

Early on Sunday morning hundreds of people appeared on the beach near the wreck collecting various items including the bodies of the drowned pigs. They were more interested in plunder than in the survivors who were clinging to the rock. For some time no amount of shouting or pleading could convince the mob to help the stranded survivors. However, finally one gentleman on the beach ascended the high cliff, about four hundred feet above the rock, while several others descended to the bottom edge of the cliff with ropes and slings. Mr John Galwey and Mr Edward Hull attempted, with the aid of a musket, to get a line onto the rock, but were unsuccessful. It was then decided to run two ropes from the cliff on the east of the rock to the cliff on the west of the rock, leaving the centre to overhang the rock. A young boy attempted to ascend the ropes to the cliff, but fell into the water and was drowned.

The survivors had to endure another night on the rock as darkness fell. Exhaustion, extreme cold, thirst and hunger made everyone silent and motionless. Morning came and Lady Roberts, with thirty men, arrived on the scene and a basket containing a bottle of wine, whiskey and some bread was lowered down. Instructions were issued to attach a further line around the rock and a cot was lowered. Mary Leary was the first passenger saved by this ingenious contraption and she was drawn through the air amid cheers. The cot was lowered continuously until everyone was removed safely. The passengers and crew had totalled fifty persons, thirty-six of whom were lost and fourteen rescued. One of the fourteen brought ashore died soon afterwards from the effects of hypothermia.

After nearly a week's recuperation, on Monday 29 January, the survivors headed for Cork in four carriages. Crowds of spectators assembled on the road to Carrigaline full of excitement and curiosity. On Monday evening at 7 o'clock, nine men and one woman arrived the South Infirmary for further treatment, while the remaining three passengers were well enough to return home.

One month later, a similar disaster almost occurred aboard the *Victory*, a steamer which departed from Cobh on 17 February 1838. On that occasion, the captain ordered that the five hundred pigs on board be thrown overboard to lighten the ship and as a result of this action, the vessel subsequently reached Kinsale Harbour safely.

Harry Badger

Over the years Cork has had numerous characters – quaint, strange and amusing. Unfortunately, when a character dies they cannot be replaced, but stories about them are retold until finally they fade, and they are ultimately forgotten. We are lucky that records of some of our most colourful Cork characters still exist. One such gentleman, Harry Badger, flourished during the 1820s. Harry spent most of his time on South Main Street near the old City Courthouse. He was very popular with the locals who constantly played tricks on him.

It seems that Harry had no taste buds and was likely to eat or drink almost anything that came his way. A few lads arranged to meet him at the local watering hole. A pint of the finest porter was paid for and given to the bold Harry. Amidst the cheers and laughter, a lively mouse was dropped into the pint unknown to the recipient. Harry downed the pint in one whip, without even drawing breath. To the astonishment of the crowd the glass was placed on the bar counter empty, with no sign of the mouse. Everyone looked at Harry waiting for a reaction, but all Harry did was give a loud burp, wipe his face on his sleeve and head for the door, smiling. He was asked by one of the lads if he had tasted anything in the porter and he duly replied 'there was possibly a fly in the drink, but that was no cause for alarm'.

The artist James McDaniel was commissioned to paint a

picture of Harry and lithographs were produced by Guy & Co. printers. He wore a brass helmet on his head which was frequently knocked off by the local rascals. To try to prevent this Harry placed a number of iron spikes on the helmet. He wore a red coat with a pair of bright yellow breeches, and was a remarkable sight. He was so popular that many artists sketched him and a number of copies of his image were reproduced on tin. These were mounted as chimney ornaments and were supplied by George Gwynne, who had a shop in the Marsh area of the city (now part of the Middle Parish).

Harry's favourite food was tripe and the larger the feed, the better. The practical jokers decided to prepare a delicious concoction in his honour. The ingredients were selected, but this was to be no ordinary culinary delight. They cut a pair of huntsman's leather breeches into tiny pieces, which were then boiled with milk, plenty of onions and a nice seasoning of salt and pepper to add flavour to the dish. They sent for Harry and escorted him to a local hayloft where the steaming pot was placed before him. The meal was so large it was reckoned that it would take several days to consume.

Harry decided to stay in the hayloft until he finished every morsel. It took two days to consume, much to the delight of the practical jokers. Unfortunately, even Harry's cast-iron constitution was unable to digest such a mixture, and it is believed that he died due to his consumption of pieces of the leather huntsman's breeches. The boys of Cork mourned him deeply, as they had lost one of Cork's most amusing and colourful characters.

Eccentric Mayor Pick

The eccentric Vesian Pick, a Huguenot immigrant from France, was elected mayor of Cork in July 1779, having previously served as city sheriff. It appears that during the French landing at Bantry Bay in 1796 he was involved in organising the city's defences. He was out of pocket as a result and received compensation of £29 14s 1d. The Lord Lieutenant arrived in the city in 1797 and was entertained lavishly by Vesian. The citizens contributed £97 7s 10d towards the expenses incurred by the Lord Lieutenant's stay and Vesian received a knighthood for his trouble. The mayor's annual allowance at the time was the princely sum of £1,200.

He never had a great grasp of the English language. When he wrote to the Lord Lieutenant during the French invasion of 1796 to inform him of the panic within the city, the opening line went as follows, 'I am writing this letter with a sword in one hand and a pistol in the other.' His introduction of the city's sheriffs to the Lord Lieutenant was just as impressive, 'Ise de Mayor your Excellency and dese are de cherubs.'

During his time in office, one of his functions was to administer judgement at the old court of conscience, an early court system where the law could be applied with clemency. He relied totally upon his clerk Walter Thornhill to advise him. Vesian, not a man to let decorum get in his way, called him 'Watty'. When any difficult cases came his way, Watty was consulted: 'What do you tink of dat Watty?'

'I think so and so, sir.'

'Well I tinks de very same', and the matter was dealt with.

If a case came to court which could not be dealt with by Vesian or if Watty was away he would say, 'Go away; de law could take no hold of dat.' An order was once given against a person for not paying a debt, and a judgement was given against the debtor's herd of cows. Having discovered that a bull was among the herd, the warrant was returned to the judge to be changed. With the Wisdom of Solomon, Vesian modified the warrant by writing on it 'one of these cows is a bull'. So with one stroke of a pen his own peculiar version of justice was dispensed.

Vesian occupied the mayoralty house (now the Mercy Hospital) and one of his duties was to entertain visiting dignitaries. Once, when a sumptuous banquet was to be provided, Watty was consulted with regard to the menu. He suggested turtle soup for a starter as he had heard that a ship was in Cobh selling turtles for about £2. Watty was immediately sent to Cobh to get a fine turtle.

During Watty's absence, a boat arrived in Cork with some turtles. A sailor arrived at the mayoralty house and Vesian met him in the hallway.

'What do you want good man, and what's dat ting?'

'Why 'tis a turtle your honour and I will let you have it cheap.'

'How much?'

'Ten shillings,' replied the sailor.

Vesian was suspicious of the low price. He had heard of mock turtle soup and, not understanding what this actually was, he flew into a rage shouting, 'Go out o' dat, you bad man, you impostor and take that nasty bird out o' dat; 'tis no turtle at all; 'tis only a mock.'

His final appearance at the municipal council was on 16 January 1821, nearly forty-two years after his election. He died shortly afterwards and was buried within the Huguenot church at French Church Street where his remains were rediscovered in the 1880s during construction work on a new heating system.

Scab Labour

A strike took place at the Cork gas works in February 1901 precipitated by three men taking an unofficial leave of absence. The men were on shift work and requested a leave of absence from the manager, who informed them that they were not allowed to leave the premises due to the heavy work schedule at the time. The men were unhappy with his decision and they promptly left work without permission.

The following morning the manager asked to see them before they resumed work, but they took no notice. At 9.00 a.m. all hands downed tools, claiming that they all had grievances and had decided to write to the directors. They eventually went back to work, but their list of grievances was sent to the directors in March 1901.

One of these complaints concerned a foreman, William Buckley, who allegedly was disrespectful to the men and was accused of petty tyranny. An example was given: on Sunday 3 March an employee, Cornelius Cronin, had his fire cleaned and almost refilled when William Buckley ordered him to empty it and start again. As a result, Cornelius had to wait until 12 o'clock for his breakfast.

The men had ten issues in total and the directors responded to each one a few days later. For example, in regard to the allegation against William Buckley, they claimed that he was always respectful to the men, although they often sorely tried his temper. In respect of the Cronin incident, Buckley said that the fire was full of clinkers, proving that it had not been properly cleaned out. Another grievance that had been raised concerned the wheeling of coal from the parish of St Nicholas to the parish of St Michael, which seemed a considerable distance. The directors, however, pointed out that the parish boundary line ran right through the works so that the men were constantly moving between the two parishes within the gas works wall. The men replied on 15 March and eventually a compromise was reached.

But on 16 May, the manager requested that an extra shovel of coal should be put on the fires in the retort house. This was seen as increasing the work load and the workers took exception to this. As a result four men were fired. Within an hour, the entire workforce was on strike again and when Mr Harrington, the manager, requested that the men return to work, they refused unless their colleagues were reinstated.

The supply of gas to the city was cut off with severe consequences. The manager, clerical staff and others took over the work and a small supply was resumed. The carters then went out in support of the striking workers and the police had to escort all deliveries to the gas works. The strikers picketed the gas works and assaulted strike-breakers who were employed by the company. They were considered the lowest form of life, and were called 'scabs' and 'blacklegs'. The strike-breakers were often imported from other areas, paid a higher rate, and were housed and fed inside the works for their own safety.

The supply of gas had nearly returned to normal when the second largest tank was mysteriously destroyed, causing havoc in the gas works. Appeals were made to the public for a fund to support the strikers, their wives and children. Cork labour leader Cornelius Lehane called a public meeting to be held on Grand Parade and leaflets were circulated urging, 'Working men of Cork assemble in your thousands and by your presence show to the enemies of labour that you are determined to maintain the strikers in their effort to resist the encroachment of the home-made capitalists. Working men unite! You have nothing to lose but your chains and the whole world to gain.'

Both sides became firmly entrenched until eventually a compromise was reached. The strike lasted until September but the strikers eventually had to accept the gas company's dictates. It took some time before life at the gasworks returned to some normality.

Two Cork Criminals

Mr and Mrs S.C. Hall were travel writers and made several tours of Ireland in the 1820s. Their aim was to give a general view of the conditions and character of the country from their own experiences. Their book, *Ireland: Its Scenery, Character etc.* was republished several times because of its popularity. Their descriptions, legends, traditions and personal sketches thoroughly charmed their Victorian readers. A critic in the *London Illustrated News* said, 'It is neither a guide book, a tale, a history or a travel book but contains instruction for the tourist, amusement for the reader, information for the student and novelties for the curious.'

The following story is taken from the Cork section of their work: Casey and Hartnett were well two well-known criminals living in Cork in 1825. They accosted a gentleman in Glanmire and robbed him of his money. A policeman gave chase and in the struggle he was killed. They were eventually captured and brought to justice. Because of their previous criminal convictions, they were sentenced to death. The gallows were erected and their graves were dug, but a legal wrangle ensued. The defendants' lawyer placed a legal challenge on the sentencing. It was pointed out that the judge in passing sentence had forgotten to add the very important words, 'And be buried within the precincts of the jail', thus technically failing to complete the due process of law. Consequently, the sentence was declared null and void.

Such was Casey's fear of death that the jailers believed he would have had to be dragged in irons and forcibly brought to the place of execution. While the judges were deliberating, Casey was hatching a plot to escape. His wife visited him in jail and brought a large oaten cake, which was inspected by the jailer. Nothing was suspected and the cake was given to the prisoner. When his wife left Casey tore open the cake and found the small file she had been instructed to hide inside.

He worked feverishly for many hours filing the iron fasteners of the bars in his cell. His plan was to free himself first and then to release his partner in crime, Hartnett, who was in the cell next door. He eventually succeeded in making an opening and after several hours of super-human effort, he was out. He freed Hartnett in the same way, but Hartnett found it difficult to follow him, as he was exhausted from the effort of forcing himself through the small escape hole and did not have Casey's stamina. He lagged further and further behind, and finally all he could do was hide in the prison yard and hope to avoid detection.

Casey climbed over two high prison walls, and escape was finally within his grasp. He reached the third wall and accidentally fell into the grave that had been dug for him. He had one last wall to scale but the brickwork crumbled beneath his feet and he fell helplessly to the ground. At that moment the prison clock struck five and he knew that his escape would be discovered, as the cells would be checked. He covered himself in a heap of dirt and waited nervously. He heard the commotion and the warders searching for him; after half an hour he was discovered. The jailers who found him said that if he had a weapon he would have killed anyone who approached him. By sheer weight of numbers, he was restrained and dragged back to his cell, a broken man. The governor, upon interviewing Casey, remarked that he was a small man to have so much strength. Casey replied, 'All great men were small men' and laughed.

After the escape had been discovered, the judges were still in session. The death sentence was thrown out and both prisoners were acquitted much to their relief. But as soon as they left the prison and entered the outside world, they were re-arrested. Casey and Hartnett were retried on the robbery charge. The sentencing judge was to have his revenge. They were both convicted and sentenced to transportation to the penal colonies for life. Justice had been done.

Priest Hunting in Cork

The earliest record of the Franciscan friary in Cork ranges from the years 1214 to 1240. It is believed that its founder was Dermot MacCarthy Mór, king of Desmond. He married Petronilla Bloet, and had a good relationship with her Norman brethren. Luke Wadding, in his *Annales Minorum*, records that accommodation was reserved in the friary for MacCarthy's private use. MacCarthy is believed to have been buried there when he died at a young age. His son, Finghen, succeeded him and he in turn continued to expand the friary. However, the family's bad luck continued when the De Cogan's and Dónal Cairbreach MacCarthy murdered Finghen in 1249. Later it is recorded that Philip de Prendergast donated a sizeable parcel of land to the friars, covering an area from the east of the city to *Tobaire Brenoke* on the west. He also bequeathed a fishery, which existed near what we now know as the North Mall, and the old distillery.

The location of the *tobair* or well was marked by a stone on one of the old walls of the Wise's North Mall distillery. The well was a place of pilgrimage for the citizens of old Cork and was reputed to have medical properties which could cure various illnesses, in particular sore eyes. Another well existed at the Franciscan Well Brewery, and flocks of people used to gather there hoping for a miracle cure for their eye ailments. However, when the friary was suppressed and the confiscated property resold, the new owner blocked up the well to stop any further pilgrimages.

Archaeological evidence unearthed at the rear of the old houses at the North Mall includes carved and inscribed stones. The historian John Windele records that in 1804 stone coffins, containing the remains of eminent nobles, knights and abbots, were excavated from the site. One of these stone coffins had a lid with the inscription in Norman French and a sceptre engraved on the lid.

The Franciscan friary is indicated on the earliest maps of old Cork, including the London Tower map of 1545. Other maps which show the site are the 1585 Trinity map and the *Pacata Hibernia* map of *c*.1600. We are fortunate that the antiquarian and folklorist Crofton Croker drew a sketch of the old friary in 1831, because five years later it was demolished.

The friary was suppressed during the reign of Henry VIII and under subsequent British monarchs. During the years 1637 until 1640, Father Francis O'Mahony, a Franciscan, records that Catholics were in control of the city, and a bishop resided in Cork. When the lord president of Munster, Sir William St Leger, took control of the city for the Protestant side in 1644 and expelled the Catholics from Cork, Donagh MacCarthy with the aid of Father O'Mahony plotted a revolt. Lord Inchiquin, Governor of Munster, heard of the conspiracy through paid informers and O'Mahony was arrested. He was tortured by his captors to extract names and details of the plot, but he remained silent. When he was hanged some of his friends immediately cut down his body from the gibbet and brought him to his sister's house in Castle Street. He was resuscitated and recovered from his ordeal, but when soldiers heard that the priest had survived, they went to his sister's house, dragged him from it and hanged him again. He did not survive the second time and his lifeless body was removed for burial.

There followed a dark period in Cork's history of informers, priest hunting and executions, until the relaxation of the Penal Laws in the late eighteenth century.

Mass Grave of 1690

During Cork's 800th anniversary celebration of its first charter of 1185, Cork Corporation took the bold initiative of creating a public park for the citizens of Cork; it was named Bishop Lucey Park and opened on 6 December 1985. Nowadays this piece of medieval Cork is often thronged with people enjoying a lunchtime break. They are happily sipping coffee and eating their lunch, unaware that underneath the park's lush growth, hides a dark secret – a huge mass grave filled with the dead of 1690.

Rev. Rowland Davies, an army chaplain with the Duke of Marlborough's forces, compiled a journal which gives us an insight into the events which occurred during the troubled times of the 1690 siege of Cork. He vividly describes the placing of several cannons far above the city at the Fair Hill end and the utter destruction of two forts near Shandon Castle. The surviving garrison retreated behind the protection of the city walls, but these old walls were no match for this new type of artillery.

Elizabeth Fort was quickly abandoned and the Duke of Marlborough's artillery exploded throughout the city. On 28 September 1690, heavy cannons were loaded near Red Abbey and concentrated cannon fire pounded the city walls mercilessly until they began to crumble. The Protestant bishop and about 1,300 Protestant inhabitants were taken as hostages by the city's Catholic defenders and used in an attempt to negotiate a treaty. However, a truce could not be agreed so hostilities broke out again, and the artillery recommenced the bombardment.

The citizens pulled up the street paving in an attempt to deaden the noise of cannon balls shattering the pavements. The cannons outside thundered and roared until they breached the wall on the east side towards Southgate. The Duke of Grafton approached over the river intending to attack the city at the breach, but a musketeer sniping from the city wall mortally wounded him, and he died a week later. The place where he fell was called Grafton's Alley (now Grafton's Lane) and is situated off the South Mall.

Naval support was sought by the attackers and the *Salamander* and another warship sailed to the marsh end. The ships' guns were aimed at the breach in the wall and cannon balls fired into the city. The defenders were also raked by small ordinance fire from Cat Fort, which was located near modern Tower Street and had a commanding view of the city. Nothing could possibly withstand this attack and the inhabitants surrendered the following morning, 28 September 1690. After the surrender, 4,000 people were confined as prisoners in places of worship.

One can only imagine the carnage, which included the rotting corpses of both humans and animals lying in the streets. As the weather was very wet, both English soldiers and Irish prisoners became ravaged by disease and died in huge numbers. The situation became so bad that some prisoners were released. The illnesses spread to the citizens and the city was soon in a dismal condition. The remains of the dead were buried in a large pit, human corpses and animals thrown in together. Because of pestilence, many traders and citizens fled to other parts of the country or went abroad.

Subsequently, when a school and alms house were being built in the late nineteenth century within the precincts of what is now Bishop Lucey park, a deep pit was discovered in which large quantities of human remains, mixed with the bones of horses, were found.

Over a period of time the stone from the old walls was removed, houses were built and gardens extended. Cork was no longer confined within the walls of its man-made boundary and its expansion brought trade and prosperity to the enlarged city.

Early River Transport

Aferry existed from Lavitt's Quay across the river to Ferry Lane, adjacent to St Mary's Dominican church on Pope's Quay, as early as 1620. On 20 March 1620, the corporation of Cork granted Dominick Roche, his executors and assigns, the sole right of a ferry boat to carry passengers into the city while the new stone bridges were being erected or for one year after the pulling down of the old timber bridges.

The next we hear of a ferry service across the Lee is an entry in the council book for the year 1713 records: 'That a fee farm [*the legal right*] of the ferries or passage boats over the north of the River Lee was granted to Edward Webber and his heirs'. The rates were set at not more than one halfpenny for a single person's passage, or for the comparable weight of a man in salt, or any other goods. The common council of the city was exempt from any charge for passage.

In 1718, the Widow Pope was allowed to build a quay between Browne's Quay and Farren's Quay to be called Pope's Quay. The area had been known as North Quay before its redevelopment. Before the building of St Patrick's Bridge, ferries were extremely important for transferring passengers, livestock and goods across the river from North Quay to Ferry Quay. The North Channel had only one bridge catering for the expanding butter and victualling trades located in the north side of the city. Smith's map of 1750 shows Ferry Quay located on what is now known as the combined area of the Coal Quay and Lavitt's Quay. The size and location of this quay area reflected the importance of the ferries for both the economy and citizens of Cork. It was not until 1774 that the real Coal Quay was first listed on a map produced by local cartographer Joseph Connor.

Before St Patrick's Bridge was constructed, ferry operators objected to the plan as they saw it as a threat to their monetary interests at the time. A public meeting was held in the council chambers on 1 May 1785 at midday, and one of the principal arguments put forward was that there was no logic to placing a bridge so near the Customs House (then located at what is now the Crawford Art Gallery). The organisers of the opposition drew up a petition to parliament which asserted that the proposal put forward would be the cause of depopulating and laying waste to thickly inhabited and flourishing parts of the city. They called for the defeat of the project which they claimed would cause the ruination of thousands. The petition was ignored and the Act for the construction of Patrick's Bridge was passed by parliament in 1786. Although clauses were inserted in the Act to compensate the ferry operators, they were informed that if they refused to dispose of and make over their rights to the ferries, a jury was to be summoned to value the ferries and they would be compulsorily acquired.

Ferry operators and Ferry Quay were of major historical, social and economic importance on this stretch of the river and for the city of Cork. These ferries operated from before the siege of Cork in 1690 and predated all of the existing bridges, the first of which, Southgate Bridge, was constructed in 1713. A ferry still operated to and from Pope's Quay in the 1920s, and my father, Denis, remembered travelling in the ferry boat with his mother as a small boy. Coal and other produce were also carried for a small fee.

Shandon pedestrian bridge has been erected near the old route of the ferry crossing, so the tradition of crossing the river near this point continues to this day.

Paying for a Title

In 1318 a royal charter established the title of mayor of Cork, a title that was to remain in use until 1900 when, during his year in office, Daniel J. Hegarty had the distinction of being both the last mayor of Cork and the first lord mayor of Cork. The title lord mayor defines the power of a city when compared to smaller towns and cities around the country. Within the Republic of Ireland only Dublin and Cork can use the title lord mayor, as opposed to just simply mayor.

Hegarty was born on 6 January 1849, the son of Daniel Hegarty senior a well-known merchant. He was an alderman of the city at the time of his election. Sir John Scott opened the election calling for a unanimous vote. This seemed highly unlikely due to the disagreements within the various political camps vying for the position, both nationalist and unionist alike. Corporation member Joseph Barrett proposed Alderman Hegarty amidst shouts of 'We do not want him', but a Mr Roche seconded his nomination and the final vote was 22 votes for Hegarty, and 19 and 14 respectively for his Corporation opponents Fitzgerald and Crean. Fitzgerald's supporters left the election in disgust and Hegarty was elected by the narrowest of margins.

Hegarty's loyalty to Britain made him a favourite of Queen Victoria and her arrival in Cork was marked by much pomp and ceremony. She conferred the title lord mayor in a royal charter issued on 9 July 1900. However, unlike his counterpart, the lord mayor of Dublin, Cork's lord mayor was not authorised to use the title 'The Right Honourable'.

The new title of lord mayor had to be officially legalised in the high court within six months and all legal costs paid for. The nationalists were totally against making the payment but Hegarty pleaded that it would be a great insult to the queen not to do so. In the end Mayor Hegarty paid the legal costs himself and became the legal owner of the charter that conferred the title.

In September 1907, Cork Corporation's legal department held a meeting concerning the lord mayor's charter which they had requested be handed over by Hegarty. However, it appears that Hegarty was giving them the cold shoulder. A letter addressed to Sir Daniel Hegarty was read out at the meeting, which outlined the granting of the charter and the legal costs which had been paid by him, £136 19s 6d. Because he had paid the fee, the patent was granted directly to Hegarty through the lord chancellor's office, making him the legal owner of the documents and title. The councillors argued that the charter should be handed over, as it was a public document. A debate then followed, and the chairman stated that he was surprised that a man in Hegarty's position should refuse to hand over the documents, as the money spent was mere bagatelle to him. Mr O'Keeffe stated that Hegarty's document was not worth one hundred and forty farthings, as he had merely a copy and not the original.

It was held that the lord mayor's charter was not worth the money paid for it and upon reading of this in the paper, Hegarty should send them the document by return post. However, the dispute was not resolved for some time, but ultimately the corporation did receive the charter.

MICHAEL LENIHAN

An Insult to Swift

Jonathan Swift, born in Dublin in 1667, was an Anglo-Irish satirist, essayist, political pamphleteer, poet and cleric who became Dean of St Patrick's, Dublin. His masterpiece was *Gulliver's Travels*, and other works include *A Modest Proposal, A Journal to Stella, The Drapier's Letters, The Battle of the Books,* and *A Tale of a Tub.* Swift was the foremost prose satirist of his day and possibly the greatest in the English language at that time, but he is less well known for his poetic ability. To hide his identity from the government he was criticising in his books, Swift originally published under pseudonyms such as Lemuel Gulliver, Isaac Bickerstaff, M.B. Drapier or anonymously.

When the British parliament decided to introduce poor quality copper coins known as Wood's coinage, Jonathan Swift wrote a series of pamphlets lampooning Wood (published as *The Drapier's Letters*). Swift's satire was so successful that the coinage scheme was withdrawn and he received the freedom of the city from Dublin Corporation because of his success in opposing Wood's coinage.

On 20 January 1736, Cork Corporation decided that he should also be honoured with the freedom of Cork. Swift had many friends in Cork, but he had also made some powerful enemies. He had insulted the merchants of Cork by insisting that instead of becoming dealers they had become peddlers and cheats. Richard Bettesworth had a particular dislike for the Dean, and it was he who had the distinction of committing Swift's printer to prison for lampooning a member of parliament. The vote taken on whether to issue Swift with the freedom of the city was not unanimous, because Bettesworth and two members voted against it.

Because of the controversy of the split vote, the mayor decided the award should be a low-key affair; the box that held the parchment conferring the freedom was not to be inscribed and the parchment itself was not to give any reason as to why it was presented. Months passed and the award of Cork's freedom to Swift became common knowledge, yet the Dean had still not been formally notified. Swift complained to the corporation: 'I am told by others as well as Lord Orrery that the city of Cork has sent me my silver box, but I know nothing of it.' He became quite agitated and threatened, 'I shall certainly sell it for not being gold.' Swift eventually received the freedom parchment, including a silver box, and his reply to the corporation on 15 August 1737 was recorded by Gerald Goldberg:

> Gentlemen I received from you some weeks ago, the honour of my freedom in a box at the hands of Mr Stannard, but it was not delivered to me in as many weeks more, because I suppose he was full of important business.

Swift was very insulted and he challenged the corporation to explain the absence of any inscription on the box and the lack of reason for its presentation on the accompanying parchment. Not even his name, or one syllable was inscribed to show that it came from the city. The box was returned with a message to either inscribe it, or give it to a more worthy person. A further month passed before the mayor had it inscribed, but without the full knowledge or approval of the other corporation members.

Swift was to have the last laugh though, because in his will he bequeathed the box to a Mr John Grattan, at the prebendary of Clonmettan with the instruction: 'That the said John do keep the tobacco that he usually cheweth called pigtail in it.' So ended the strange events surrounding Dean Swift and the freedom of Cork City.

Muskerry Tram Crash

The Cork and Muskerry Railway was developed to promote tourism in and around the Blarney area. Because it ran along the roadway from Western Road to the Carrigrohane Road, it could be called a railway or tramway. It was affectionately known as the 'Muskerry Tram' to Cork citizens, although it was also known as the 'Hook and Eye'. It carried passengers, livestock, farm produce, coal and other goods and the city railway station was located at Bishop's Marsh, now Jury's Hotel.

The railway opened on 8 August 1887 and one week later 2,000 passengers were carried to a sports meeting in Blarney. Owing to the large turn-out, the 2 p.m. train was packed to capacity and had difficulty moving due to the heavy load. Eventually it was able to proceed, but at a very slow pace.

The success of the 'Muskerry Tram' led to the opening of a Coachford extension and this was followed by a Donoughmore extension in 1893. First-class passengers had the luxury of umbrella stands in their coaches and fires were lit at the waiting-rooms of Coachford, Peake, Kilmurray and Blarney during the cold winter months

The 'Muskerry Tram' was widely used by the city's commercial travellers, and farmers and businessmen alike carried produce in both directions. Children's excursions, angling, golfing trips and picnics were all catered for, ensuring the financial success of the railway. The original locomotives proved inadequate and two new engines, No. 5 Donoughmore and No. 6 The Muskerry, were commissioned. The locomotives on the line had their own identities namely the Donoughmore, The Muskerry, City of Cork, St Anne's, Peake and Blarney. Unfortunately, all the names were removed when the Great Southern Railway took over the line in 1924. The Donoghmore went to the Tralee and Dingle Railway and The Muskerry was transferred to the Schull-Skibbereen Tramway. In 1954, it ended its long working life and was scrapped.

Quite a few accounts of the train on the Muskerry railway were written by local writers and John C. Coleman gives us this description: 'Leaving the station the train took to the Western Road and with much clanging of bell, leisurely puffed its way westward.'

The train was never noted for its speed. Coleman's

father told him of an incident near Peake on the Coachford branch when, returning from a fishing trip, the train passed them. The engine-driver saw them running down the hill and leaning out of his cab said: 'Take your time boys I will oil her at Peake.' In 1905, a labourer was charged with the offence of leaving the carriage while the train was still in motion. The evidence showed that the defendant fell from the train as it was leaving the station, even though the train had been stopped for a full ten minutes beforehand and he had had ample time to disembark if he wished. He received a cut on his head and it was stated that he had been under the influence of drink at the time. He was fined the princely sum of one shilling, but had to pay an extortionate amount of court costs to the sum of ten shillings.

A moment of glory came when the Muskerry tram was in collision with a steamroller at Inchigaggin in 1927. The headlines in the newspapers announced that it was the only train in the world ever hit by a steamroller. At the time, a stretch of roadway was being resurfaced near Carrigrohane, when the Donoghmore locomotive and two coaches were derailed by the impact. Ambulances raced to the scene but the only casualties were a few elderly ladies who had fainted. The steamroller came off worst in the incident as the collision blew the huge roller off its bearings and it collapsed to the ground. Locals joked that the steamroller was racing the train. It was a sad day for everyone when on Saturday 20 December, 1934, the last train left Western Road for Blarney. People turned out in their droves to say goodbye to their old friend the 'Muskerry Tram'.

Cork's Silent Transport

An early cartoon postcard of 1898 gives us an insight into the consternation expected with the arrival of the electric tramway to Cork City. It was forecast that these mobile horseless carriages would wreak havoc on the streets. Horses would run amok, carriages overturn, women faint and pedestrians would be forced to run for their lives. Those boarding the trams would be crushed in the onslaught to board. On Monday 12 December, 1898, the *Evening Echo* recorded: 'Every now and again the distinctive clang of the tram bell is heard and it is a good thing that the public are accustomed to giving up the middle of the roadway in good time because it will make matters so much easier when the trams are in full running order.' The prediction that horses would become upset was correct as the *Echo* chronicles: 'The other day one of the Constabulary horses violently threw its rider because a tram came along.'

The opening date of 22 December 1898 was scheduled to coincide with the Christmas festivities in the city. Eighteen trams were purchased for the opening and further units were to be acquired with the expansion of the routes. Such was the demand that the trams were filled to capacity and members of the public had to wait for the next service. The routes were: the Statue (Patrick's St) to Summerhill, the Statue to Gaol Cross on the Western Road (every twelve minutes), the Statue to Tivoli, and Blackpool to Victoria Road (every ten minutes). The longest distance was the Statue to Douglas (every twenty minutes).

There were some teething problems and minor accidents were recorded. A Blackpool tram went out of control and crashed into the bottom of Murphy's Brewery chimney shaft, a tram was derailed at the end of Summerhill, and the Douglas tram was involved in a collision at Patrick Street. Some inebriated Cork citizens celebrating the Christmas festivities fell off the trams but, overall, there were no serious incidents.

The official title of the tramway provider was the Cork Electric Tramways and Lighting Company Ltd., a London branch of the powerful British electrical suppliers, Thomson-Houston. A large electrical generating station was constructed at Monarea Marsh near Albert Quay. Edward Fitzgerald, a leading Cork builder, who was later instrumental in establishing the Cork Exhibition of 1902, built the powerhouse. The chimney stack of the station was one hundred and thirty feet high and it survived, as a city landmark, for many years until it was blown down by a gale. The trams were only a small part of the main operation as the generation and supply of electricity to the city and surrounding areas proved lucrative for the company. However, an enormous amount of money and investment in technology was spent on the tramway system.

The trams ran for a period of thirty-three years and were capable of carrying between forty-three and forty-eight people seated. Because the routes were fixed and trams were cumbersome and slow-moving, new technology in the form of buses became popular. The Electricity Supply Board, following the establishment of the Shannon Hydroelectric Scheme, was in a position to take over the electricity generating facility and its customers, and in 1931 the Cork Electric Tramways and Lighting Company Ltd. went into voluntary liquidation. The deadline for closure was 31 March 1931 and the routes were to be taken over by the Irish Omnibus Company. As the bus fleet proved very inadequate the trams received a six-month reprieve.

The end finally came on 30 September 1931, amidst the noise of foghorns and the brilliant colour of fireworks. The citizens of Cork bade a sad farewell to their old friends, the Cork electric trams. The memory of the old Cork trams is recorded to this day, as Tramway Terrace in Douglas commemorates the route of the Statue to Douglas tram.

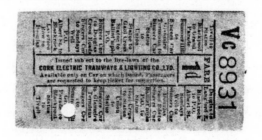

James Barry, Female Surgeon

It is said that the truth is often stranger than fiction as the following story certainly demonstrates. The date of Margaret Bulkley's birth is uncertain, but sometime between 1789 and 1795 seems the most probable. The family house was at Georges Street (now Oliver Plunkett Street), and was listed in *Connor's Cork Directory* of 1824. The family was closely related to James Barry, the well-known Victorian artist and Margaret was his niece.

In a letter to her brother who was fighting in the West Indies, Margaret wrote that, 'was I not a girl I would be a soldier! However I must honestly confess that I would prefer a sword to a musket and I should like a pair of colours, at least then I should use them to promote myself.'

In 1809 with the aid of her mother, a bold scheme was hatched and Margaret enrolled at Edinburgh university as a male medical student, as women were not allowed to study medicine at that point. Margaret now disappeared from the face of the earth forever and James Barry was born. In order to keep up the deception, all contact with friends and family were cut. Barry graduated from Edinburgh in 1812 and enlisted in the British army in 1813, becoming the first female MD in Britain and Britain's first female officer, unbeknownst to her employer. By 1816, Barry had risen to the rank of assistant surgeon to the garrison of Cape Colony in South Africa.

She became the personal physician to the governor of the Cape, Lord Somerset, and it is rumoured that they had an affair. Barry was promoted to medical inspector of the colony due to Somerset's influence. Suspicions were aroused as to Barry's sex but her bad temper soon put paid to any such rumours. In fact, Dr Barry fought several duels when her voice, manner or professional conduct was called into question.

A clergyman once sent a message to Barry requesting her to extract a tooth. Considering this an insult to the profession, Barry sent him a blacksmith who told the clergyman that he had come to pull his tooth. She had several clashes with the authorities and was sent a summons for defamation, which she tore to shreds, stating: 'If I had my sword when Mr Fiscal suggested sending me to jail, I would certainly have cut off both of his ears to make him look smart.'

Whilst in the Cape she succeeded in improving the quality of water and sanitation facilities for soldiers, although fighting for better conditions for the soldiers often resulted in making enemies. Barry also recommended wine baths for some of her patients, and believed that these could reduce the risk of certain infections.

She also became renowned for her sympathetic treatment of women patients, which led to some speculation about her gender. One female patient said of her, 'No man could show such sympathy for one in pain.' Barry performed the first successful caesarean operation in South Africa, although her only previous experience of this particular procedure was from reading about it in a book. In honour of the good doctor, the boy's happy family christened him James Barry Munnik.

Barry's bad temper coupled with rumours of being Lord Somerset's homosexual partner forced a return to Britain in 1828. Following this she served in Mauritius, Trinidad and the island of St Helena, where her ill temper again caused trouble with superiors. Sailing from St Helena and returning to Britain without official leave she was reprimanded, but she cheekily retorted that the journey was for the purpose of a haircut. Florence Nightingale was insulted by Barry and later stated: 'He was the most hardened creature I ever met throughout the army.'

In 1845, Barry contracted yellow fever but recovered and in 1857 was in Canada with the rank of Inspector General of Hospitals. In 1864, forced into retirement by her age, she returned to England, where she died from dysentery in July 1865.

Sophia Bishop, the maid who laid out the body, discovered that Barry was indeed a female. She sold the story to the *Manchester Guardian* and it was printed on 21 August 1865. The army responded by sealing all records connected to Barry for a hundred years. Dr Barry was buried in Kensal Rise cemetery, London with name and rank engraved on the headstone. Recently family letters have surfaced which prove beyond all doubt that Dr James Barry was indeed a woman.

A Letter Writer

Recently a letter came into my possession, which was written on 18 May 1871 and gives us a traveller's insight into the city's activities at that time. Thomas Oakley was writing to his father at the Railway Hotel, Killarney, informing him of his experiences in the city of Cork. Upon leaving Queenstown and arriving in Cork, he soon discovered that all the hotels were full to overflowing and he could not obtain a room anywhere. He eventually found a vacancy at a private guesthouse and he recorded a thoroughly enjoyable stay there. He observed that the city was crowded to capacity, as men, women and children had arrived from all parts of the country to attend a three-day horse-racing event. Because he had never witnessed such a major horse-racing festival, he decided to go along. Thomas attended a flat race, a trotting race and a steeplechase. He had never seen finer horses and was very impressed with their power and speed. He was surprised to see so many intoxicated people, not only of the working classes, but also the better sort, as he himself says.

The following morning he visited Blarney Castle and Dr Barter's water cure establishment at St Anne's Hydro, which promoted the use of Turkish baths as beneficial to health. He also stopped at a factory near the castle and was taken on a tour of the woollen mills. The proprietor brought him to his house and grounds where he was made most welcome and found his visit enjoyable. He wrote that the woollens were of a very high quality and that this excellent stock would sell at 1s 8d per yard at London and was a very soft material. Thomas was surprised to find mills in Ireland that could easily surpass English quality.

This letter gives an impartial insight into the social history of Cork City. Horse-racing and the festivities associated with it were very popular. People with the money and interest were prepared to travel from afar to participate. Drinking to excess appears to have been a problem for both the rich and poor. The success of a temperance crusade led by Father Matthew earlier in the century had clearly weakened following his death. The initial procession of people taking the pledge to abstain from alcohol had lost its momentum because there was no shepherd to lead the flock away from temptation.

Hospitality was the order of the day and Thomas Oakley clearly enjoyed his stay in Cork. After his enjoyable trip, one can only wonder if Thomas made a return trip to Cork and wrote more complimentary letters about the beautiful city.

The Bibliophile Bishop

Bishop John Murphy was one of Cork's most celebrated book collectors. He was born in Cork in 1772 and was a member of the Murphy family of Catholic merchants. His brother James was one of the founders of Murphy & Co. distillery. At the early age of fifteen years, John was sent to Paris to further his education and study for the priesthood. After two years, he was forced to return home due to the upheaval caused by the French Revolution. He subsequently continued his studies abroad at the Irish College in Lisbon and was ordained a priest in 1794. In 1797, he became curate of St Peter and Paul's church in Cork and within a short period became parish priest of the surrounding diocese. He was consecrated Bishop of Cork in 1815. Bishop Murphy's rise to prominence can be attributed in no small way to his influential family connections.

The Bishop was afflicted with a chronic form of bibliomania, namely he could not resist collecting books, and he scoured the countryside in search of them. He was apparently quite a wealthy man in his own right apart from his stipend as Bishop of Cork; the census returns for the Shandon area in 1820 record that he was the landlord of forty-six properties in Skey's Lane in the parish of St Mary's.

A good library at the time was the measure of a gentleman's wealth, good taste and education; immense sums were spent procuring expensive books and lavish bindings to impress fellow collectors. Bishop Murphy often visited Dublin on his book buying sprees and the booksellers were eager to sell their wares to this compulsive buyer of good books. Patrick Kennedy, who had a bookshop in Anglesey Street, recorded in his diary a contemporary account of the Bishop's arrival in Dublin:

> At last the anxious guardian of past literature is gladdened by the apparition of the gold-headed cane, the silk stockings fitting in the buckled shoes, the waistcoat not innocent of snuff, the loose coat, the broad brimmed hat, and the kind good natured face under it.

After greetings had been exchanged and the bookseller's family received the Bishop's blessing, the serious business of book dealing could be conducted:

> If a price was asked which he affected to think was too high, he would stop short, gaze ludicro-sternly over his spectacles at the culprit and cry out: 'Ah? You think to impose on the poor Connaughtman [*sic*].' He made up his bill as he went along; and when he left the shop, he left behind him cheerful words and something to meet the rent or the auctioneer's bill.

Indeed the Bishop's reputation spread far and near. A number of notable travel writers made it their business upon arriving in Cork to call to meet him. Charles de Montalembert notes in his account from 1830 that he was tired of rushing around trying to locate Bishop Murphy whom he eventually found to be a fat little man, joyful and very intelligent, who spoke fluent French. In 1843, Johann Georg Kohl gives us a vivid description of his library:

> The Roman Catholic Bishop of Cork has one of the most interesting collections of books I have ever seen. This learned and industrious man has turned his whole house into a library: not only has he converted his sitting-rooms and dining-rooms into book-rooms, but even in his bedrooms, every available space is filled with books. His attendants, even his maidservants, sleep in little libraries; the staircases are lined with books along the walls; and the corridors, which lead from room to room, have

full bookcases at their sides; everywhere books are literally piled up, even to the garrets.

The Bishop had the largest private library in Ireland which contained many fascinating and costly works. In 1846, he visited Rome and returned with £200 worth of books to add to his enormous collection. He commissioned many Cork poets to write poems in Irish in manuscript form and fortunately, the manuscripts have been preserved in the library at Maynooth University.

The *Southern Reporter* newspaper reported the death of Bishop Murphy on 1 April 1847: 'The malady from which he died and under which he had long suffered, was water on the chest.' His remains were enclosed in a cedar shell, upholstered and lined with white satin. The shell was placed in a lead coffin, weighing over two hundred and fifty kilograms, which was then sealed with solder. The lead coffin was then put into a solid oak casket, covered with rich purple velvet and gold-plated mountings. Contemporary accounts of the funeral describe huge processions of mourners entering the cathedral; indeed the galleries of the cathedral had to be strengthened by additional supports to cope with the weight. Shops and public buildings were closed as an entourage of over eighty clergy and a long line of carriages containing the gentry of all religious persuasions solemnly followed the cortège to his final resting place. Bishop John Murphy, the bibliophile Bishop, had gone to the great library in the sky.

His dying wish was that his collection would remain intact and be housed in Cork. But after his death, the

auctioneer's hammer fell to the highest bidder and the library was scattered to the four corners of the world. Indeed, the collection of upwards of 70,000 books was so large that it took a year to auction and many of the books were sold off by weight. Bishop John Murphy had amassed one of the greatest collections of books in Ireland in his lifetime, which to this day has never been surpassed.

A Mayor Hanged

In 1491 a young man, Perkin Warbeck, arrived in Cork from Lisbon. He was the servant of a Breton silk merchant, Pregent (Pierre Jean) Meno. Warbeck noted that people in France, on seeing him dressed in the silks of his master, took him for a person of distinction, and insisted that he must have been either the son of George, Duke of Clarence, or the illegitimate son of Richard III. He began to give himself the title Richard, Duke of York, and proclaimed himself the younger of the two 'Princes in the Tower'. He claimed that he was permitted to escape when his brother was murdered. His story appeared plausible at the time and was accepted by those who wished to overthrow King Henry VII. Several prominent people in Cork supported his claim as the rightful heir to the throne of England. John Walters, a well-known merchant and mayor of Cork, threw his full weight behind Warbeck's campaign to claim the title. Warbeck also obtained the support of Ireland's most powerful men, namely the Earl of Kildare and the Earl of Desmond.

In an attempt to build a power base, he besieged the city of Waterford, but when the town resisted he was forced to withdraw. After a short time, he decided to gather an army to invade England with help from the King of France, travelling to France for that purpose. During this period France was continually at war with England. The French king, Charles VIII, seized the opportunity to cause mischief and to try to place this important ally on the throne of England. Unfortunately for Warbeck a peace deal was subsequently brokered between France and England effectively ruining his chances of French support.

Subsequently he fled from France to Flanders where Margaret, Duchess of Burgundy, and an enemy of Henry VII, declared he was her rightful nephew. With her help, he mustered a small army of six hundred men, and set sail for Kent to raise support for his cause. The landing was a complete failure with one hundred and sixty of his soldiers captured and then executed. He returned to Cork in 1496 to raise support, which was not forthcoming, and then turned his attention to Scotland. In Scotland, Warbeck was well received. He married a daughter of the Earl of Huntley, Lady Catherine Gordon, and was granted a monthly stipend of £112. James IV also supported his claim to the English throne, hoping to cause problems for his hated enemy Henry VII. In September 1496, a Scottish invasion of England was planned in support of Warbeck, but resulted in failure and the Scots withdrew without even meeting the English forces. The incursion served as an excuse for Henry to raise taxes for the defence of the realm. Warbeck was now an embarrassment to the Scottish king, and he fled once more to Ireland.

On 26 July 1497, assisted by the Earl of Desmond and a small band of one hundred and twenty soldiers, he headed for Cornwall, encouraged by the King's rising unpopularity, due to the draconian tax increases which had been administered on the population. Soon his army swelled to 6,000 men and upon reaching Exeter, he burned the North Gate and forced his way through to the East Gate, but was fiercely resisted by the citizens. The following day he continued the attack, and two hundred of his men were killed. Hearing of the approach of the royal forces and the fact that a price of 1,000 marks had been put on his head, Warbeck fled.

He was soon captured and in his confession to Henry at Taunton on 5 October 1497, Warbeck admitted that he was the son of a middle-class merchant of Tournai, Belgium. He was kept prisoner in the Tower of London but when, in 1499, another pretender, the Duke of Warwick, attempted to overthrow the King, Henry acted quickly. Perkin Warbeck and his ally John Waters (Mayor of Cork) were tried at Westminster by a jury of twelve men, and found guilty of high treason. They were hanged at Tyburn and their heads were spiked on London Bridge as a warning to others. Rumours persisted that Perkin Warbeck's face was disfigured from beatings before his execution to ensure that he bore no resemblance to the Duke of York. The charter of the city of Cork was forfeited because of the rebellion of the mayor and its citizens. But a new charter was granted to the corporation of Cork on 1 August 1500.

The Waterloo Glass Factory

The city of Cork had a glass-making factory which rivalled any in Ireland or Britain, the Waterloo Glass

Factory. Founded by Daniel Foley in 1815, it was located on Wandesford Quay, and its name commemorated the famous victory of the Duke of Wellington over Napoleon at the battle of Waterloo. An early reference to Foley is recorded in Connor's *Cork Directory* for the year 1812, a commercial directory listing Cork's prominent citizens and merchants. *The Overseer*, a bi-monthly periodical, of 24 December 1816 had this to say of the new venture:

> By his forming of the Waterloo Glass House Company which is now at work, Mr Daniel Foley is giving employment to more than one hundred persons. His workmen are well selected, from whose superior skill the most beautiful glass will shortly make its appearance to dazzle the eyes of the public and to outshine that of any competitor. He is to treat his men at Christmas with a whole roast ox … They have a new band of music with glass instruments and they have a glass pleasure boat and cot and glass net which when seen will astonish the world.

At this time the company was making bottle and flint glass, although shortly afterwards they were engraving and cutting glass. The company installed the latest steam engines to drive the cutting machines, which gave a greater degree of precision than was previously possible with the old hand-turned equipment. The Waterloo Glass Factory was quick to adopt new methods such as annealing which made glass more durable and heat resistant. Apart from selling plain and cut flint glass, they also sold tumblers, lamps and wine glasses. The main markets for glass in the city included the army, the navy, taverns, hotels, the resident nobility, gentry and the better-off citizens of the region.

From 1825 onwards, Irish manufacturers had to pay

duty on all the glass they produced. Because of increasing competition from mass-produced glass in England the company was forced to reduce its prices by 20 per cent in 1829. Daniel Foley entered into partnership with local merchant Geoffrey O'Connell in 1825 and this arrangement lasted until 1830, when Daniel Foley retired from business. The factory was put up for sale in 1830 and 1831. *The Cork Constitution,* November 1831, announced the recommencement of the Waterloo Glass Factory under the sole ownership of Geoffrey O'Connell. In 1833, he too decided to retire from business, but by 1834 he was again involved in glass-making. Unfortunately, the venture was short-lived and in 1835 the gates of the factory were finally closed for good. Geoffrey O'Connell was declared a bankrupt, a direct result of excessive excise duties on Irish glass.

The Cork Constitution, 18 June 1835, carried the following advertisement:

> An Auction for the non-payment of excise duties of splendid cut and plain glass at the Waterloo Glass Works, Clarke's Bridge until the entire of the splendid stock is disposed of, consisting of rich cut decanters, salad bowls, celery and pickle glasses, dessert plates, dishes, tumblers, wine glasses of every description, hall staircase globes, side lights and water crofts. After the stock is sold, the household furniture of a house in Mardyke Parade is to be auctioned.

Finally, in March 1836 the Cork auctioneer William Marsh advertised the actual premises in Wandesford Quay for sale. This was the final episode in the illustrious history of the Waterloo Glass Factory.

The Cork trades association felt sufficiently aggravated by the penal glass duties (especially in view of the Waterloo Glass Factory closure) to send a petition to parliament in 1835. They complained that the duties on flint and cut glass were disproportionate to the means of the working class and the agricultural population, making glass at least twice the price it had been before the imposition of the duty. According to the petitioners when window panes were broken, they were simply not replaced. An example was given of one street in Cork City where 194 windows which had been designed for 2,212 panes, had 72 per cent of these panes either broken, blanked or boarded up with timber. The excise duty on glass was removed in 1845 but by that time, the Irish glass industry was non-existent.

Today Waterloo glass is highly prized and much sought after by collectors because of its beauty and rarity.

Tales of a Rake

Charley Crofts was born in Velvetstown, County Cork, on 1 January 1771, the seventh consecutive son of William Crofts. Around the time of his birth, his father William was a respectable country gentleman with good property which he inherited from his ancestors. However, Charley was to take after his uncle George, who was fond of humour, practical jokes and mischief. George was also quite fond of the drink and lived until the ripe age of ninety-two, unlike Charley's father, a water drinker, who died at the early age of fifty-four. Charley's education was foremost in his father's mind and he had high hopes that his son would become a doctor. Unfortunately for William his son neglected his education and spent his time robbing orchards, playing practical jokes and lampooning his teachers.

Following his father's death, the property and effects were auctioned and the family moved to Cork city. Charley was sent to school once more, but was expelled and his mother Elizabeth had him apprenticed to Keven, Izord & Co., merchant chandlers. Owing to the smell of grease and tallow, and his dislike of work, he left and became an employee of Mr Litchfield, a linen draper in North Main Street. One day, on returning to his residence on Bachelor's Quay, he discovered water had flooded the house, and the wine bottles from the cellar were floating about. When the servants had gone, Charley quickly gathered up the wine bottles. Once the tide had abated and the water in the house retreated, he invited his friends to a party before his mother's return. When the wine was finished, the bottles were to be smashed in an attempt to pretend they were broken in the flood. The bottles were flung against the wall in different directions and the fragments fell to the ground. His mother arrived to inspect the damage and knowing her son's reputation, her suspicions grew. The cellar was scrutinised, bottle necks were collected and it was discovered, much to his dismay, that no corks existed in the remains of the bottles. Charley quickly fled the scene of the crime and his mother's temper.

When the 1798 rebellion broke out in the country, the authorities, including the gentry of the city, decided to form a yeomanry corps to protect their property and families. Charley was one of the first to enlist and obtained the rank of corporal. Brigadier Major Barry was on a tour of inspection and the corps went to Captain Wallis' castle at Drishane for a military drill. Obeying orders as a soldier was his first duty and disposing of a few bottles of good claret every night was his just reward.

The city having returned to normality after the rebellion, the yeomanry corps was disbanded. One night at a party, Charley met Mr Seymour, the manager of the Cork theatre, and during the evening, wishing to demonstrate his vocal talents, he warbled the 'Groves of Blarney'. So impressed was the theatre manager that he declared that if sung in the same way on stage a full house would be guaranteed. The next day Charley went to dine with his family and informed them that he was to go on stage. They asked him to change his name so as not to bring disgrace on the family, but he refused. A family meeting was arranged, with everyone subscribing money to bribe Charley not to take to the stage. The sum of £50 was agreed upon and thus ended his short-lived career as a singer.

The appearance of the last will and testament of his father William Croft was to have far-reaching consequences for his son. The family had conspired and succeeded in preventing Charley from receiving his fair share of his father's will, namely the head lease of Ballyhea worth in excess of £300 per annum. This revelation occurred in the year 1815 some years after the death of Charley's mother and eldest brother. Having approached the remainder of the family, a friendly arrangement was not forthcoming. In Cork, three eminent lawyers were consulted who agreed with the legality of the claim. Legal proceedings were instituted and one year's income was quickly swallowed up. Money was running out fast and Charley had no option but to relinquish his claim. He went to Cobh to live and appealed to his brother, the Rev. William Crofts for the sum of £20 to pay his debts, but the request was refused.

One way of paying off his debt was to write a book *The Memoirs of Charley Crofts* and allow public subscriptions for this to flow in. Family secrets were to be exposed, much to the embarrassment of surviving relatives and friends. The Croft family intervened and offered to pay the sum of £20 per year for life, if the work was not published. Time dragged on with no sign of payment, while outside interest in the book waned. It was believed that the publication would never appear but Charley finally published his memoirs in 1829.

Cork Arctic Explorer

Jerome Collins was born at 50 South Main Street, Cork in the year 1841; his father had a lime and salt works (the site is now occupied by Beamish's Brewery). Jerome became a civil engineer and in 1864 was appointed clerk of works during the construction of the old wrought iron

North Gate Bridge. When the bridge was completed, Jerome went to America.

There he applied his talents to weather forecasting. He became friends with Gordon Bennett, the owner of the *New York Herald,* who was keenly interested in the science of predicting weather systems. By studying weather patterns, Collins was able to predict what was coming and so extreme storm warnings could be cabled by the *New York Herald* to the Irish and English papers, sometimes up to ten days in advance, which was an amazing feat at that time.

In 1878, Lieutenant George Washington de Long wanted to find a new route to the North Pole so he asked Bennett if he would provide financial assistance. Jerome became involved and his talents proved invaluable to the expedition. An ex-British gunboat was purchased and renamed the *Jeanette.* The vessel was strengthened to withstand the huge pressures of icebergs in Arctic waters at a cost of $500,000. It was loaded with enough provisions to last three years. The total crew including officers comprised thirty-two men, and, unlike previous Arctic explorations, this expedition was to travel through the unexplored regions of the Bering Strait.

By the middle of September 1879, the ship had become completely encased in ice not far from Herald Island. For many months, Jerome Collins and his companions remained trapped in the ice-bound ship. Temperatures at night fell to below -40 degrees, freezing the mercury in the thermometer. Under these intense and severe pressures, one of the crew went insane. Soon the second winter was approaching and there were only fifty-three tons of coal left on board.

On 11 June 1881, still trapped, the deck of the *Jeanette* buckled under the great pressure of ice and the ship was doomed. It had to be evacuated and all hands were put to work rescuing provisions, clothing and medicine. Everyone managed to escape onto a large ice floe, bringing life-boats and sleighs with them and at 4 a.m., the ship sank into the icy sea.

For four terrible months, the men wandered in the desolate frozen wilderness. The sun's rays eventually thawed the snow and ice so much that the sleighs could not travel in the slush. Life-boats and sleighs then had to be pulled over the dangerous terrain. Finally, they came to a fork in a river and three members of the party went to explore one branch of the river whilst the others made their way along the second route. One group, led by chief engineer George Melville, eventually made their way to a settlement in Yakutsk, Russia, in January 1882. The survivors, with the aid of the natives, tried unsuccessfully to locate the second party.

A second expedition was financed by the American government to try to find de Long, Collins and the remaining crew. It left New York for St Petersburg, and was aided by the Russian government on humanitarian grounds. De Long's body was eventually discovered beneath the snow, in a remote uninhabited region of North-East Russia. The last entry recorded in his diary, 30 October 1881, stated that Collins had died at his side. It also recorded how de Long, Collins and their comrades had killed and eaten seals to stay alive, but later had had to resort to chewing parts of their deerskin trousers and to killing and consuming the last dog travelling with them in an attempt to stay alive.

The bodies were brought by reindeer-drawn sledges over a distance of eight hundred miles across frozen snow to Yakutsk and then by horse-drawn sledge over 4,900 miles to Orenburg in Sweden. The coffins were taken by rail to the German port of Hamburg and then by ship to New York and on to Cork. So began the longest funeral in the world covering a distance of 14,000 miles.

A solemn requiem mass was celebrated at St Coleman's Cathedral, Queenstown (Cobh), on 8 March 1884 and the cortège left by boat for the Marina in Cork City. The day was very wet and stormy, but the citizens turned out in their thousands to see the funeral proceed through the streets of Cork. The burial took place at Curraghkippane graveyard overlooking the River Lee, about three miles from the city. In a sermon given by the Very Rev. Dr Hutch he said: 'His body was brought home to his native city, mourned by two worlds, and nature herself shed a kindly tear upon his bier while the storm winds sang a parting requiem over his grave.' The only headstone facing north in the graveyard of Curraghkippane is a Celtic cross marking the final resting place of Jerome Collins, an Arctic hero from Cork.

The Paper Man

John Francis Maguire, born in 1815, was the eldest son of John Maguire, a Cork merchant. His father steered him towards a career as a barrister, and during his studies for the legal profession he made frequent contributions to the newspapers and periodicals of the day.

On 10 April 1830, Father Mathew, the renowned temperance campaigner, addressed a large group of campaigners at Blackamoor Lane and the Cork Total Abstinence Society was born. The *Cork Standard, Southern Reporter,* and the Protestant paper *The Cork Constitution* all reported this famous event. The newspapers of the day were not slow to see the advantages of spreading this new gospel of temperance, with the growing interest in the movement increasing their circulation.

John Francis Maguire, who was also quick to see the benefits of allying himself with this new movement, became editor of the first temperance newspaper, *The Cork Abstainer*, owned by William Thompson, a member of the Total Abstinence Society. Published every Saturday, it sold for the princely sum of 2*d*. The first edition, 20 February 1841, stated its principles and advocated the cause of national temperance for all creeds and classes through total abstinence. Eighteen issues were published, and the final edition on 26 June gave notice that *The Cork Abstainer* was to cease publication to be replaced by a new newspaper.

On 30 August, the first *Cork Examiner* appeared on the streets. It was allied to the repeal movement founded by Daniel O'Connell, the Liberator. Maguire stated that 'his new journal would stand or fall upon the honesty with which its columns are devoted, not to serve private or personal ends, but for the welfare and interests of the whole community'. It was published on Monday, Wednesday and Friday at the exorbitant price of 4d.

Maguire qualified as a barrister in 1843, and following his successful foray into the world of newspaper editing which included *The Cork Total Abstainer* and the *Cork Examiner,* he became a recognised authority on Irish current affairs. In 1852, he became MP for Dungarvan for a period of thirteen years. From 1865 until 1872, he represented Cork as MP. A Repealer and Irish nationalist, he was elected mayor of Cork for the years 1853, 1862, 1863 and 1864. He was also involved in founding the first Cork Exhibition of 1852. He was the author of many books including *The Irish Industrial Movement* (1852), *The Life of Father Mathew* (1863), *Rome and its Rulers* (1856), *The Irish in America* (1866) and *The Pontificate of Pius IX.* His novel, *The Next Generation* (3 vols), advocated women's rights and he was a supporter of suffragettes. He died on 1 November 1872 at his residence, Ardmanagh, Glenbrook, and he was buried at St Joseph's cemetery, on Tory Top Road.

His son, John Francis Maguire junior, appears to have had no interest in the publishing business and subsequently became an actor. He played comedy roles for many years under the name John Francis. He produced the Gilbert & Sullivan opera *Patience* for the benefit of the Mental Asylum. It was extremely successful and with the help of Sir John Arnott, a well-known philanthropist, further performances were staged at the Assembly Rooms on the South Mall in Cork City.

The *Cork Examiner* subsequently passed into the hands of the accomplished journalist Thomas Crosbie, whose family are still proprietors of the newspaper.

The Outlaw Art Ó Laoighre

O n the sad occasion of the cold-blooded murder of her husband Art Ó Laoighre, Eibhlín Dubh Ní Chonaill composed one of the most important and moving poems in the Irish language, *Caoineadh Airt Uí Laoghaire*. An English translation of a verse of the poem is as follows:

> You poised for a canter,
> On your slender bay horse
> The Saxons bowed to you
> Not for love of you
> But for deadly fear of you
> Though you lost your life to them
> Oh my soul's darling

Art Ó Laoighre served in the Hungarian army and when he returned home, his fellow countrymen held him in some awe. He was renowned for his strength, skill and agility. He rode around the countryside on a beautiful white horse. Ó Laoighre was a Catholic, who had amassed considerable wealth and owned several fine racehorses. One day at the Macroom races, his horse won a race ahead of a horse belonging to Abraham Morris. Morris was a magistrate and powerful landowner of the ascendancy class who was jealous of the esteem in which Ó Laoighre was held by the public.

Morris was angry because his horse had lost, especially to a papist, and he later sent a messenger to Ó Laoighre with the sum of £5 to purchase the winning animal. Under the terms of the Penal Laws, a Catholic could not own a horse over the value of £5 and had to surrender the horse upon being offered that value. Ó Laoighre replied that he would die rather than give up his horse to Morris. Legal proceedings were instituted and Ó Laoighre was declared an outlaw under the terms of the Penal Laws.

Morris sent for the militia and the soldiers were ordered to shoot Ó Laoighre on sight. An ambush was laid for Ó Laoighre at an old ruined house near Macroom, and two soldiers lay in wait for their quarry. When Ó Laoighre approached shots were fired, but they missed their intended target, whereupon Ó Laoighre returned fire. He shouted at his servant to make for home with his horses but the soldiers had reloaded and fired again. This time the musket shot hit its target and Ó Laoighre fell dead from his horse. His horse took flight and when it arrived at his house riderless, his wife, Eibhlín Dubh Ní Chonaill, instinctively knew he was dead. Because of the public outcry, Morris eventually stood trial for the killing of Art Ó Laoighre, but was acquitted.

The Penal Laws prevented Ó Laoighre's burial inside the confines of Kilcrea abbey. For some years, his body was buried in a field nearby until finally he was reburied in Kilcrea cemetery. Art's brother decided to seek revenge and when he discovered that Morris was in Cork, he travelled there with a loaded gun. Morris was staying at a Mr Boyce's house in Peter's Street. Conflicting accounts exist concerning the assassination attempt on Morris. One version, by the antiquarian John Windele in 1837, states that Morris was standing near a window and the fatal shot entered under his ribs and he died. Another states that having escaped the attempt on his life, Morris offered a reward of a hundred guineas for the capture of the assassin. Newspaper accounts of the period seem to support this theory and it appears likely that Morris survived the assassination attempt but was badly shaken by his ordeal. Fearing further attempts on his life, he sold his possessions and vanished into obscurity.

Art's brother escaped to France on board one of the many smuggling vessels which operated from West Cork or Kerry. A story was told that the fugitive had a narrow escape whilst in France whereupon he said that if he had stayed in Cork, he would have been lengthened on the gallows, but in France he was in danger of being shortened by Madame Guillotine. Eventually he took a ship to America and he lived there to a ripe old age.

Peter Levi, Professor of Poetry at Oxford, referred to the lament for Art Ó Laoighre as the greatest poem written in these islands in the eighteenth century. His wife composed the following epitaph for his tomb:

> Lo! Arthur Leary, generous, handsome, brave,
> Slain in his bloom, lies in this humble grave.

Abducting an Heiress

The lively tune 'Merrily Danced the Quaker' has its origins in the abduction of a young Quaker heiress in Cork by Sir Henry Hayes, the son of Mr Atwell Hayes, scions of a well-known Cork family. Atwell Hayes was quite eccentric and on one occasion entered a ballroom in a miniature state chariot pulled by an enormous hairy goat. The goat became a favourite amongst the citizens of Cork, where he roamed freely and lived to a very old age. A saying existed at the time, 'As old as Atty Hayes' goat', which was used to describe an elderly person. Atwell's son Henry was to come to public attention for very different reasons altogether.

Sir Henry was widowed with several children and was a very popular figure in Cork. Unfortunately for him, his expenses exceeded his means, so he hatched a plot to abduct a wealthy heiress. Even to attempt such a crime carried the death sentence under existing laws of the time. The victim selected was Mary Pike, the only child of Samuel Pike, a Cork banker, who had died some time previously and left his fortune of £20,000 to his only daughter. Her mother lived in the city centre but was in extremely poor health.

In July 1797, Mary Pike, then aged twenty-one years, was staying with her relative Henry Cooper Penrose at his house, Woodhill, on Lovers Walk. On 22 July, Sir Henry Hayes visited the house on the pretext of viewing the magnificent gardens. Mr Penrose entertained his unexpected guest and Sir Henry lingered in the gardens until dinner-time. Accordingly, he was invited to dinner although he was unknown to Penrose before his visit. Sir Henry sat near Miss Pike and appeared quite enamoured with her.

During the conversation, he gleaned information that Dr Gibbings was Mary's mother's doctor. Subsequently he wrote a letter to Dr Gibbings seeking information on a medical matter. The doctor duly replied in his own handwriting which Sir Henry copied for his own deceitful purpose.

Having carefully copied the doctor's handwriting he sent a forged letter to Mr Penrose stating that Mrs Pike had suddenly taken ill and that she wished to see her daughter, as she had not many hours left to live. The letter was timed to reach Woodhill after midnight. Miss Pike, accompanied by Henry's daughter, Miss Penrose, set off into the darkness in the family carriage. It was a wet and stormy night and they had not travelled far when armed men stopped them. Miss Pike was kidnapped and driven off under an armed escort towards Vernon Mount, the Hayes family home.

Then, mysteriously, the horses stopped at the bottom of the steep avenue and refused to go any further despite any amount of coaxing and cajoling. Sir Henry jumped from his horse and carried the struggling woman towards the house. A man was present in the house, dressed as a clergyman, and he performed some sort of marriage ceremony. A ring was forced onto the finger of the unwilling bride who broke loose and threw it on the floor. Sir Henry reacted in the rudest manner, shouting that Miss Pike was now his wife.

Miss Pike was eventually allowed by Hayes to write a letter which she addressed to Mr Penrose telling him of her plight. Sir Henry knowing that the game was up took flight and a reward of £1,000 was offered by the government for his capture. Several years passed until Sir Henry entered the premises of his old friend Mr Coghlan, a hairdresser on the Grand Parade. As pre-arranged with Hayes, Coghlan informed the authorities, Sir Henry was arrested and the reward was claimed by his friend. The trial date was set for 13 April 1801 before Mr Justice Day. The trial proceeded and after a few hours' deliberation the jury found the prisoner guilty, but recommended mercy. The death sentence was commuted to transportation to New South Wales. Hayes arrived in Sydney in all his finery on a ship named *Atlas* – he had bribed the captain to receive special treatment which included having his own personal valet. Because of his social status, he acquired some land and built a house named Vaucluse. It is said that he imported earth from Ireland and legend has it that no snakes existed on his land.

He spent over twelve years in Australia before he received a pardon, due to his daughter's chance meeting with the Prince Regent. She was invited to a ball given by the Prince at the Pavilion, Brighton, when she caught his eye with her good looks and dancing skills. She presented a petition for her father's release which the Prince granted. Sir Henry returned to Cork but was shunned by society and the fairer sex. He died in 1832, aged seventy, and was buried in the family vault in the crypt of Christchurch, Cork. So ended the colourful career of Sir Henry Hayes of Vernon Mount, Cork.

Bull-baiting in Cork

The barbaric practice of bull-baiting had its origin in England. It involved capturing a bull, which was then tied to a stake and attacked by trained bulldogs. The bull was placed in a specially constructed arena and tied to an iron stake so that it was only able to move in an area of about thirty feet. The object of the sport was for the dogs to bring the bull to a standstill. The bull's snout, the tenderest part of his body, was often filled with pepper to enrage the animal thus encouraging it to toss the attacking dogs in the air. Wagers were often placed on the winning animal, which promoted the sport among the rich and poor alike. Another form of this so-called sport was called bull-running, where men and women tormented the poor animal making horrendous noises, terrifying the bull, pursuing him and finally beating the poor creature to death.

In 1770, a contemporary newspaper account records that inhuman savages forcibly removed a bull in the north side of Cork City, and that he was driven through the city streets by savage dogs. The poor creature was then baited in the south of the city. Driven mad with fear and rage, the bull broke loose and charged back into the city forcing the citizens indoors and shopkeepers to close their premises. The bull was eventually trapped near Broad Lane (now the site of St Francis' church) and was baited by dogs at the Exchange near Castle Street. The spectators were armed with sticks and the unfortunate bull's torment lasted for a further five hours. The account recorded that four frightened pregnant women had fits because of the occurrence. A horse was tossed several feet into the air by the bull; a crippled beggar also became airborne and landed in a kennel. Eventually, the poor animal, worn out from his exertions and persecution, dropped dead.

The practice of bull-baiting appears to have taken place in all of the major cities of Ireland. A Dublin newspaper report of 20 November 1749, reprinted in Tuckey's *Cork Rembrancer* of 1837, has the following paragraph:

> Several persons were committed to Newgate for taking bulls from poor countrymen and driving them mad about the streets of Dublin, to the great detriment of their owners, and the hazard of the lives of the inhabitants of that city.

The majority of the inhabitants of Cork City at that time believed that the savage amusement of bull-baiting should cease. The practice was seen as uncivilised, devoid of humanity by the citizens and shocking to foreign traders and visitors. However, another incident occurred in 1770, when a tormented beast was driven through Cork's Main Street, Castle Street and the quays for a considerable time much to the terror of the people. A man was thrown into the air by the bull and narrowly escaped death.

The custom of bull-baiting had become so widespread that country people were afraid to travel to the market with their bulls. If they were taken from them, they received no compensation whatsoever for their livestock. Finally, in

1835 the British parliament passed the Cruelty to Animals Act which expressly forbade the keeping of any house, pit or other place for baiting or fighting any bull, bear, dog or other animal.

The Rebels

Henry Sheares senior was a Cork banker whose private bank was located at the corner of Moore's Street, to the rear of the Mercy Hospital. He was a well-known figure in literary circles and frequently contributed articles to William Flynn's *Hibernian Chronicle*. However, his family are remembered because of his sons' involvement with the United Irishmen. Henry junior, who was the elder brother, was forty years old in 1798, with a large family to support. The younger brother John was thirty-two years old and was engaged to be married to a Miss Steele. John had an annual income of £3,000 per year and his fiancée complained that he spent most of it on books.

On 19 May, just four days before the 1798 rising was planned to take place, Lord Edward Fitzgerald was informed on and arrested. Just three days were to pass before John and Henry Sheares were also arrested. The Sheares brothers had been members of the United Irishmen for at least five years before their arrest. John contributed to the United Irishmen newspaper whilst his brother Henry was an organiser. Henry was first introduced to his betrayer, John Armstrong, by J. Byrne, a United Irishman and bookseller of seditious material. Henry was suspicious of Armstrong and subsequently avoided him, but not before introducing him to his brother John. Unfortunately John was completely taken in by Armstrong and was soon sharing his plans for an attack on Dublin Castle with him.

By 20 May, Armstrong had become so friendly with John that he was invited to join his family for dinner. Armstrong played with the children whilst at the same time plotting the downfall of their father. Because of his seniority within the United Irishmen, John had access to all the plans for the rebellion. Armstrong informed the authorities and the two brothers were arrested. A trial was hastily arranged and John Philpot Curran, a notable barrister, was employed as their defending counsel. Curran hoped to exploit technical flaws in the case, but the prosecution became aware of his plans and was ready for him.

Everything possible was done to blacken the character of Armstrong, a professed atheist and perjurer. But John Toler, the infamous Lord Norbury, was determined to pass the death sentence on the two brothers. John Sheares instructed Curran to do everything possible to protect his brother and was quite prepared to lay down his own life to achieve this. John pleaded for Henry's life but to no avail. The trial, held in Dublin, was a marathon session lasting over twenty-one hours with only a twenty-minute interval. The brothers were convicted of high treason and Lord Norbury pronounced the death sentence.

Whilst in custody Henry wrote a letter pleading for clemency, to be delivered to the lord chancellor. The messenger was delayed by a series of unfortunate events and when he eventually reached the place of execution at Green Street with a letter of respite, he was too late. He saw the executioner holding Henry's decapitated head, shouting 'behold the head of a traitor'. The two brothers were buried in the crypt of St Michan's church in Dublin and legend has it that their bodies have never decayed.

As for the informer Armstrong, he received his thirty pieces of silver in the form of a fine fat government pension of £500 per year. This reward was not just for betraying the Sheares brothers, but for exposing the entire plans for the 1798 rebellion in the country to the relevant authorities.

Poems and songs were composed in memory of the Sheares:

> We saw a nation's tears
> Shed for John and Henry Sheares
> Betrayed by Judas Captain Armstrong
> Forgive we cannot yet
> And never shall forget
> The memory of the friends that are gone, boys gone
> Here's to the memory of the friends that are gone.

It was not until 1898, the centenary of their death, that Nile Street, Cork, was renamed Sheares Street in honour of the patriotic brothers. The Sheares brothers' legacy provided the inspiration for further heroic insurrections in Ireland.

Early Aeronautics in Cork

The first hot air balloon to carry passengers in a basket was named *Aerostat Réveillon* and was launched on September 1783 at Versailles. The passengers comprised one sheep, one rooster and one duck, and the balloon remained airborne for the grand total of fifteen minutes before crashing to earth. King Louis XVI of France originally decreed that condemned prisoners were to be used as guinea pigs for these pioneering experiments, but this was later rescinded. The first manned attempt was in November 1783 when Joseph and Étienne Montgolfier flew their balloon over Paris for around twenty minutes. Only five months after this first successful balloon launch, the balloonists turned their attention to Cork. One can only assume that the geographical location and weather conditions of Cork were ideal for this new form of aeronautical transport. On 27 March 1784, a hot air balloon ascended near the Mardyke at approximately 4 p.m. much to the curiosity of the huge crowd of spectators. This successful airborne adventure finished at 6 p.m., having covered a total distance of eighteen miles.

Before its descent it was seen by John Moynihan, a curious resident of the district, who observed this bizarre apparatus floating high up in the sky. He was quite convinced that it was the work of the devil, but his curiosity made him follow it to its landing spot. He had never heard of these wonderful flying objects before and when he saw flames coming from the tube at the end of the balloon, he was certain that it was Lucifer himself about to land. Shortly afterwards he observed that the 'demon' had landed between two rocks and had been secured by strong ropes as if it was a prisoner. The airmen brought it back to their residence and the neighbours, having heard of this weird flying machine, gathered in numbers nearby. A spark subsequently landed near the inflated balloon causing the flammable gases to explode, making a sound louder than thunder and a man and a woman were badly burned. There was consternation, and people desperate to escape this fiery monster ran away as quickly as possible. Several women fainted and those who ran to safety were convinced that they had escaped from the fires of hell.

This first account of a balloonist flying over Cork had ended successfully, for the occupants at least. Unfortunately, in May 1785, a balloon crashed in Tullamore, County Offaly, resulting in a fire that burned down about one hundred houses. This tragedy was probably the world's first aviation disaster.

A further account exists of the magnificent men in their flying machines on September 1816. A gun was fired to announce that a Mr Sadlier was due to ascend from the barrack yard on Military Hill in a hot air balloon. The balloon passed over the city where it was observed that flags were being waved. Mr Sadlier threw out some ballast to ascend higher, and after about twelve minutes disappeared into a cloud, becoming invisible for a time.

Sadlier provides this account, reprinted in Tuckey's *Cork Rembrancer* of 1837:

> I ascended at twenty minutes before five o'clock with the wind blowing moderately from N.W.N.; the balloon on first rising had an unpleasant motion, but soon became steady; being now nearly perpendicular over Cork. At ten minutes before five, the balloon entered a thick cloud when the city and the county became obscured from me; the balloon was now completely inflated.

It was flying quite high over Cork, with views of Bantry and Waterford being observed by this brave aeronaut. His plan was to land near Ringabella, but upon descending, he 'became stuck in a grass enclosure and rebounded into the nearby fields'. The grappling hooks secured themselves into a hedge and the balloon then landed safely. The owner of the farm, Mr Hodder, appeared and observed this unusual apparatus on his land but he stayed out of harm's way until he felt that it was safe to come closer. A servant of Mr Hodder's next appeared with a group of friends and invited Sadlier into his master's house. The balloon and equipment were then gathered up for safe-keeping. A nearby resident, Mr Foote, provided refreshments and a horse so that Mr Sadlier could travel to Mr Hodder's residence. Upon his arrival at the house, the triumphant aviator was given food and lodgings. There he was fêted and treated with the utmost respect and kindness until his departure the following morning.

Healthcare for the Poor

On 10 July 1787, a public dispensary was established to supply medical advice and medicine free of charge to the sick poor of Cork City. This dispensary was located at Hanover Street in the centre of the city. The service was to be paid for by donations and subscriptions from wealthy citizens on a voluntary basis. Any persons found to be suffering from fevers or other acute illness which confined them to their homes, could be admitted on the recommendation of a benefactor or subscriber. The official figures from its commencement in 1787 until 13 April 1791 were 12,462 patients admitted. Six doctors and two surgeons were appointed to this establishment. The resident apothecary was paid the handsome salary of £70 per annum. The operating costs of running such a large private institution must have been enormous, especially if its only source of revenue came from voluntary contributions from the wealthier citizens of Cork.

Apart from providing for the sick poor, another charity, the Humane Society, was founded to provide help for persons who had suffered from near drowning experiences. This society worked hand in hand with the dispensary's doctors and staff. It appears that some form of equipment was kept in readiness for the sole purpose of reviving any unfortunates who had been rescued from the river. When the medical committee or resident physician received notification of the rescue of such individuals, payments were made to the citizens who aided in the rescue. The apothecary of the dispensary was then summoned so that everything possible could be done to aid the recovery or resuscitation of the patient. Connor's *Cork Directory* for the year 1812 provides the following information, 'Within the last twelve months 4,670 [*sic*] patients were received.'

The medical committee comprised six doctors, namely Dr Fowler, Dr O'Brien, Dr Sharkey, Dr Osborne, Dr Lindsay and Dr Lloyd. The treasurer was Mr G. Young, the secretary Mr M. Roberts and the apothecary was Mr Boyle Travers. By 1846, the title of the institution had become The General Dispensary, Humane Society and Cow-pock Institution, which was supported by subscriptions, donations and grand jury presentments. Cow-pock was used as a natural vaccine to control the outbreak of smallpox and the dispensary was inoculating patients and citizens alike. An official committee governed the dispensary. An annual subscription of one guinea was the amount needed to keep two patients on the books. Any person contributing ten guineas was elected to be a governor and was entitled to recommend four persons as patients at any time. Because of their status, subscribing clergymen of all religious persuasions were entitled to double privileges.

Mr J.W. Topp was the secretary in 1846 and was also secretary of another charity, the Indigent Room Keeper's Society. The objectives of this society were to visit the sick and distressed poor in their own homes, give charity to the needy and where possible obtain gainful employment for those concerned. In 1867, it was recorded that no city of equal size to Cork responded to the call of charity more than the wealthy inhabitants of Cork. Another charitable body, the Society of St Vincent de Paul, had already by then spent over thirty years administering to the poor. Other Cork institutions which existed at the time were: The Blind Asylum; a reformatory; Ragged Schools; a refuge; a penitentiary; orphan asylums; and asylums for aged and necessitous females. Several alms houses, a host of sick poor and other merciful societies also existed which claimed to take care of the wants of all who needed their assistance, irrespective of their creed.

One of Cork's oldest surviving charities, the Sick Poor Society, was founded in 1853 to look after the needs of the less well off. It continues to provide financial and other support to those in need across the city to this day. In 2007, the Cork branch of the Sick Poor Society distributed over €112,000 in cash and coal, and its members made over 3,000 family visits. The society's work is carried out confidentially, without publicity and is funded through house-to-house collections, donations and bequests.

Buried Alive

S t Peter's church is located at North Main Street and was one of the most important ecclesiastical sites in the city of Cork as early as the twelfth century. It is currently the home of the Cork Vision Centre. This area is steeped in history as an early map of Cork, the *Pacata Hibernia* map from *c*.1600, clearly shows St Peter's church and its adjoining laneway with tower in situ.

The early church was a gothic structure containing several small chapels and oratories. Its historic importance is recorded by such major events such as the election of the Lord Lieutenant of Ireland. Tuckey, in his *Cork Remembrancer* of 1837, states that in 1381 the Bishops of Ossory, Cork, Cloyne, Lismore and Waterford and Limerick, the Earl of Ormond and Mayor of Cork assembled at St Peter's church. The unanimous decision of the delegation was the election of John Colton, Dean of St Patrick's and Lord Chancellor of Ireland, to the position of Lord Lieutenant of Ireland. But by 1683, the church had lost its importance and had fallen into some disrepair; the old belfry had to be demolished completely and rebuilt.

Despite the decline in the church's fortunes, the most influential of Cork families continued to be buried in St Peter's graveyard over the following centuries. The oldest memorial tablet inside the church records the burial place of Mary Hartstonge and the following inscription is quite legible:

> Here lyeth the body of Mary Hartstonge
> Being daughter to Capt Roger Bretridg who
> Died in the eighteenth year of her age on the
> 2nd day of January 1674

On the same wall Zachary Cook, a merchant of Cork is

recorded as 'departing this life' on 23 March 1707 aged 67. However, earlier headstones existed in 1750, when historian Charles Smith visited the church and found gravestones dating back to 1500. In the 1970s, the burial site was moved near a recreational park in Grattan Street and these headstones were repositioned near the boundary wall.

In 1753, it is said that Francis Taylor was buried in St Peter's and the next morning was found sitting up in his grave, his cap and shroud torn to pieces. His coffin was broken, one of his shoulders much mangled, his hands full of clay and blood was observed running from his eyes, because he had been buried alive. By coincidence, a Joseph Taylor published a book in 1816 entitled *The Danger of Premature Internment, Proved From Many Remarkable Instances of People Who Have Recovered After Being Laid Out for Dead, And Of Others Entombed Alive.* This book was a bestseller which took advantage of the widespread fear of premature burial. Was this author a relative of the Francis Taylor buried alive in Cork in 1753?

In 1713, a school was established by the church for the education of forty schoolchildren of the parish who were to be clothed and taught to read and write. The salary paid to the teacher and mistress was the princely sum of £14 per annum. The school existed solely because of the support generated by donations and bequests from its local benefactors.

In 1782, the old church was demolished to make way for a new building. Whilst St Peter's was being rebuilt, the railings and figures of the Deane family vault were removed for safekeeping. Unfortunately, for the Deane family some opportunistic thieves struck and stole the lead coffins of Sir Matthew Deane and his wife. (In 1722, Sir Matthew Deane had donated funds to establish an almshouse in the parish of St Peter's to be administered by Thomas Deane.)

The new church was completed in 1788, but the foundations could not support the heavy metal belfry and it had to be removed. By 1816 the church walls had bulged considerably and the parishioners considered it unsafe to attend service. Down through the years many modifications were carried out to strengthen its walls and foundations. Having served the people of Cork for over eight hundred years, St Peter's was deconsecrated in 1949. After its deconsecration, it was used as a warehouse for storing furniture and was badly neglected and heading towards dereliction. Fortunately, it attained a new lease of life when it was restored and transformed as the Cork Vision Centre.

Abandoned Babies

In 1735 an act was passed for establishing a workhouse in Cork, this was similar to the act which was passed in Dublin in 1703. The Cork Act also made provision for the rebuilding of the cathedral church of St Finbar's as well as for the construction of the foundling institution. Its objectives were to employ and maintain the poor, and provide for the education of foundling children. The money for this venture was to be raised by taxing all coal coming into the city. A duty of 1s per ton was placed on all coal imported, for a term of thirty-one years.

It was reported that exposed or foundling children in several parishes of the city were so numerous that they frequently perished for want of care. Some institutions placed a basket outside where a baby could be placed and thereby have a better chance of survival. Additional revenue was collected from weigh-house fines, carriage licences and penalties on car drivers.

Abandoned children proved to be a very vexing problem for the authorities in Ireland and Britain. The perception existed that unwanted children born out of wedlock were immoral and this social stigma placed them at a terrible disadvantage. Their parents were usually poor, badly educated and were at the bottom rung of the social ladder. It was also widely believed that helping these children would only encourage further unwanted pregnancies and encourage prostitution. The cost of the upkeep of the foundlings was enormous: food, clothing and education all had to be provided and paid for by taxation.

The Cork Foundling Hospital was opened on 12 March 1747; it was located on Leitrim Street on what is now the site of Murphy's Brewery. There were two ordained ministers of the Church of England assigned to the hospital. These ministers held no other position, so they could concentrate solely on their duties – to convert the foundlings to the Protestant faith. Three guineas were paid to the boys or girls who served their apprenticeship faithfully and who attended church service regularly. They were also required to attend the Protestant schools of their parishes for instruction.

So widespread had the practice of abandoning children become that in the early 1800s Cork was described as the gathering place for all the bastards of the south of Ireland. A barbaric ritual was the branding of the infants under the arm; this was done so that in the event of the child dying another could not be substituted by its family in its place. The institution was filthy, sickness was widespread due to overcrowding and morale was extremely low. The mortality rate was extremely high. Between 1820 and 1833, of 3,247 inmates admitted, 2,018 of these children died. Rev. James Hall, in his tour of Ireland in 1807, records that three hundred children were then incarcerated in the hospital.

Children put into the care of the institution had to be nursed, clothed and taught to read and write. The infants could be placed with foster mothers until they reached the age of six or seven, when they then became inmates. More importantly they were to be brought up in the Protestant religion. They were exchanged between the Cork and Dublin institutions to prevent any interested relatives from hindering this religious policy. When the number of males became too large, and because of limited finances, the male children were apprenticed to trades until the age of twenty-one when they were discharged. Failing this, these boys were sent to work on ships or they became household servants for a period of up to seven years. The main advantage to the authorities was that they had a cheap pool of labour to call upon, especially in time of war.

Samuel Lewis' *Topographical Dictionary of Ireland* in 1837 describes the buildings of the Hospital as 'a small quadrangle of which the chapel forms one side, the other three are approximate to school rooms (two for the boys and two for the girls), dormitories and other necessary apartments'. In 1854, a parliamentary paper was published outlining the expenditure of the institution since 1843. A statement from the Poor Law Commissioners declared that the institution was no longer required and that it was to be sold off and the proceeds to be divided between various charities. On 13 July 1843, there were 283 males and 407 females from 5½ to 12 years of age resident. By March 1854, plans were well advanced to abandon the building. According to the *1854 Report on the Foundling Hospital*, the sum of £500 was paid for the transfer of five imbecile foundlings to the Cork District Asylum. These unfortunates were Catherine Grant, Sarah Anderson, Anne Beresford, June Rose and Margaret Hanley.

The following table from 11 August 1854, shows the number of children who had been claimed, apprenticed or who had left the institution, or who were deceased since 13 July 1843:

1843		Male	Female	Total
13 July	Number in Establishment	283	407	690
Since Decreased as Follows				
	Apprenticed	106	116	222
	Emigrated	67	171	238
	Died	53	67	120
	Eloped	21	---	21

Discharged Servants	---	7	7
Struck off at Nurse	20	9	29
Sent to Lunatic Asylum	---	5	5
Superannuated	---	2	2
Claimed	0	0	0

Number Remaining, 11 August 1854			**46**
From 16 to 20	14	25	39
From 20 and Upwards	4	3	7

PART I.

No. 1.—RETURN showing the several PAYMENTS made as COMPENSATION to and in the PURCHASE of ANNUITIES for Retiring Officers during the Year ending March 1854, with the NAME, AGE and PERIOD of SERVICE of each.

NAME.	AGE.	OFFICE.	PERIOD OF SERVICE.	AMOUNT OF ANNUITY.	SUM PAID FOR ANNUITY.		
			Years.	£.	£.	s.	d.
Charlotte Collins - -	74	Schoolmistress -	26	20	137	8	7
Luke Donovan - - -	56	Schoolmaster - -	38	20	240	14	6
Mary House - - -	63	Infirmary Matron -	31	12	131	19	6
Mary A. Harvey - -	50	Infirmary Servant -	26	10	158	—	1
Maria Russell - - -	42	House Servant -	14	10	183	1	1
				Exchange,&c.	2	3	—
					853	6	9
			Period of Service.		Amount of Compensation.		
Bridget Watkins - -	38	Schoolmistress -	17	- -	£. 200	—	—

No. 2.—RETURN showing the SUM paid to the CORK DISTRICT LUNATIC ASYLUM for the reception of Five Imbecile Foundlings, during the Year ending March 1854.

Names:

1. Catherine Grant   -   -   -   -   ⎫
2. Sarah Anderson   -   -   -   -   ⎪
3. Anne Beresford   -   -   -   -   ⎬ £. 100 for each.   -   -   -   £. 500.
4. Jane Rose   -   -   -   -   ⎪
5. Margaret Harley   -   -   -   -   ⎭

Of the forty-six remaining, two had become paid servants; their names were William Alexander and Susan Newman.

It is sad to note that of the six hundred and ninety souls admitted not one single child was claimed by even one of its parents. This institutional system ensured that these abandoned children survived but at a high price. They became pawns in sectarian politics, had no quality of life and most died at a very young age never having seen their parents.

Steeple Ready to Fall

The site of the church at Christchurch lane is one of the oldest inhabited parts of the city and possibly dates back to the Viking era. Records exist that date the earliest parish church of the Holy Trinity to 1185 and several churches have been built there over the centuries. The oldest bequest to the church was made by John Wynchedon whose will of 1306 left one mark to the church, while twelve pence was given to each priest and two shillings to the clerk. He also bequeathed the sum of twenty shillings each year to the rector and vicar so a 'likeness of the crucifixion scene is made'. This scene was to be made of wax gilt, five pounds in weight and two candlesticks were also to be provided for the great altar.

Christchurch was the main place of worship in the city, and the corporation used it officially. In the early seventeenth century, the church was used as a place of worship by French Huguenot refugees, before the building of their own church on French Church Street. During the siege of Cork in 1690 by the Duke of Marlborough the church suffered badly from cannon fire and one shell even came through the roof. But the city's defenders caused more damage by removing stone from the church, as pavements were pulled up and used to repair the gaping holes in the city walls. After the siege, 4,000 prisoners were imprisoned in the County Courthouse, St Peter's church and Christchurch.

After the siege of Cork the church was in a terrible state of disrepair, and the corporation repaired the gallery in September 1691 as it was used almost exclusively by the mayor, sheriffs, aldermen and the burgess of the city. Christchurch was an extremely important landmark in Cork City and a clock was installed in the tower so that the citizens could see the time all over the city. In 1702, the clock in Christchurch steeple was officially called the town clock. When it stopped working the corporation ordered that it should be repaired and the bill sent to them. Joshua Slocomb, the principal clockmaker in the city, was employed to repair the clock. The chamberlain paid him the sum of £3 sterling for the initial work and twenty shillings per year to keep it in good repair. In 1706, Richard Deeble had become the official clockmaker and he was admitted as a freeman of the city for his services. When the Exchange was built in 1708, Deeble installed a new clock in this commercial building. After this period the Christchurch clock lost its importance, as it was no longer the principal time-keeper in the city.

The present-day church was completed in 1720 as the siege-damaged building was finally demolished in 1716. The present building was designed by the architect John Coltsman and the tower rose one hundred and thirty feet above the city. The building costs were paid for by a tax of one shilling per ton on all coal and culm (coal-dust) brought into the city. The steeple was completed in 1726 but because it was built on a poor foundation, it sank completely on one side. This subsidence was an on-going problem and the church had to be taken down as far as its roof and rebuilt in 1748. The historian Charles Smith refers to the church in 1750 and states that it was referred to as the king's chapel. Various accounts of the church in the late 1700s refer to its leaning steeple and an old Cork saying was 'All to one side like Christchurch'. Lord Chief Justice Willis described the leaning tower as being in danger of falling on three or four houses and was, 'A terror to everybody that passed along the street.'

Various improvements and modifications were made to the building and in 1825 the architect George Pain submitted new plans but these were rejected as being too costly. The new façade and entrance were added in 1827 at a cost of £3,500 6s and in 1828 the interior was totally renewed. Unfortunately during the zealous rebuilding of 1828, every memorial was dislocated and many were destroyed.

The church was not confined to being just a place of worship; it was also a public place of punishment. The vestry books survive and one of the entries for November 1729 records that a pair of stocks were to be made immediately. These stocks were to be used to punish offenders on the Lord's day during the times of divine service. The location of the stocks is given as, 'Ye said stocks be placed by ye gate of ye said church.' The stocks survived for at least thirteen years, as another entry for August 1742 records that the sum of £2 8*d* was paid to Mr Cooke for a pair of new stocks and for other joinery work within the parish of Christchurch. The church was deconsecrated in 1978 after centuries of worship and Cork City Council then purchased it. Appropriately, it housed the Cork Archives Institute until recently.

The Bard of the Lee

John Fitzgerald was born in Hanover Street, Cork, in 1825. His father died when he was four years old, leaving his mother to rear him and his other siblings. He was educated at Father Mathew's school at Blackamoor Lane, Sullivan's Quay school and the North Monastery. Upon leaving school, he became an apprentice to his brother-in-law Michael Murphy, who had a successful cabinet-making business in London. Having worked there for a year, he became homesick and returned to Cork. He obtained a new position in the chemistry department of Queen's College (now University College Cork) as an assistant to Doctor Blyth. This position did not suit him, so he returned to his former trade of cabinet-making, with Cornelius O'Keefe whose factory was located at Grattan Street. These premises later became home to the Cork Mechanics Institute.

Upon completing his apprenticeship, he became an accomplished wood carver. He became a teacher at the Cork School of Art and he was supervisor of the wood carving department at the Dublin Exhibition of 1853. His talent as a wood carver was further recognised when he won first prize at the Cork Exhibition of 1883. Fitzgerald was also a proficient watercolour painter, but his real genius lay in his poetry and prose. He was but twelve years old when he wrote his first poems, and two other Cork poets, Thomas Condon and Daniel Casey, were fellow pupils in his class. Thomas Condon's principal work was 'Gilla Hugh or the Patriot Monk' and Daniel Casey's 'Cork Lyrics' was a very popular humorous work.

In 1892, Fitzgerald wrote a very informative article entitled 'An Account of the Old Street Ballads of Cork' for the *Journal of the Cork Historical and Archaeological Society*. He had listened to these old ballads hundreds of times as a child and he recounted them from memory. Fitzgerald recalled that in 1842 Mr Haly, the printer in Hanover Street, then a very old man, was still printing ballads with his own woodcut illustrations. Richard Caulfield, the antiquarian, considered these ballads so important that he sent several examples to the British museum. By coincidence, Fitzgerald recorded that Haly's ballad sheets were found by a schoolmate of his in an old log hut in a remote part of Colorado. The three songs that he found were 'The Green Linnet', 'Nell Flaherty's Drake' and 'Brennan on the Moor'. These ballad sheets were mass produced and printed on poor quality paper, as a result very few examples have survived. Many of these sheets had no printers' name and so are unidentifiable today, making Fitzgerald's research invaluable.

Fitzgerald had a particular fondness for local history and he knew every historic nook and cranny in the city. He painted topographical drawings of houses and bridges around Cork in sepia and watercolours. It is believed that he drew in the style of the painter Nathaniel Grogan. He chronicled every event worthy of note as either a story or a poem. He wrote several comprehensive articles for the *Journal of the Cork Historical and Archaeological Society*. Fitzgerald's books include *Legends, Ballads and Songs of the Lee* published in 1862 and *Echoes of '98: a memoir of the rebellion of the United Irishmen in Cork*. He loved Cork with a passion and he continued writing up until his death at eighty years of age. He was buried in St Joseph's cemetery with his fellow poets Thomas Condon and Daniel Casey.

One verse of his satirical poem written in 1862 about the Berwick Fountain is worth reprinting:

Judge Berwick – God bless him! Ah, how could he tell?
The five hundred he gave would give us such a sell;
For before it was finished, twelve hundred it cost –

But mavorne! All the labour and money was lost;
For it scatters the water that comes from its top,
And 'twill wash down your shutters, thus saving a mop.
When it works, try to pass it with shiny silk hat,
And 'tis clear of the fountain you'll keep after that.
Try a new suit of tweed, as a masher, a swell,
And their fountain will make you remember it well;
It falls (like the rain) on just and unjust,
So 'tis seldom the residents growl about dust.

It is quite appropriate that three of John Fitzgerald's water-colours are hanging in his former place of work The Crawford Art Gallery. These are depictions of Elizabeth Fort and Old St Finbar's in 1796, the South Gate Bridge in 1797 and Old Blackrock Castle, Saluting the Corporation in 1724. He left behind him a rich legacy of poetry, historical notices and charming paintings of his beloved Cork City by the Lee.

Cork's Greatest Collector

Robert Day was born on 12 January 1836 and was the son of Robert Day senior, a Cork merchant. Robert was educated at Mr Hamblin's and Dr Porter's private school in Cork. He excelled at school and he showed a particular love for history. The family firm of Robert Day senior was founded in 1831 and it quickly became one of the finest saddlery and harness manufacturers in Ireland. Their magnificent premises at No. 103 Patrick Street had a splendid double frontage with high lofty plate glass display windows. The factory to the rear at Nos 3 and 4 Bowling Green Street employed a large staff of qualified workmen engaged in making every requirement for the equine trade. Also made on the premises were trunks, hat-cases, travelling bags, clipping machines, horse clothing, rugs, knee caps, bandages, whips, spurs, walking canes, riding and driving coats, aprons and leggings – in fact everything for the stable, paddock or hunting field could be purchased on the premises.

Upon leaving school, Robert joined his father's firm where he quickly rose through the ranks. On 1 December 1857, he married Miss Rebecca Scott, the daughter of Robert Scott, a wealthy Cork merchant. Day became chairman of Robert Scott & Co. Ltd, wholesale hardware manufacturers and merchants. He was an alderman and justice of the peace, and in 1893 he became High Sheriff of Cork. He was appointed trustee of the Cork Savings Bank and the South Infirmary Hospital, and he became a director of the Commercial Buildings Company.

But his main interest was the study of antiquities and he became involved in the historical societies of Cork, and further afield he was a fellow of the Royal Numismatic Society and a fellow of the Royal Society of Antiquities. He was president of the Cork Literary and Scientific Society, Cork Historical and Archaeological Society and a member of the Royal Irish Academy to name but a few. He contributed several articles on historical and archaeological subjects to many learned societies and was editor of the much enlarged reprint of Dr

Charles Smith's *The Ancient and Present State of the County and City of Cork* (1893).

Over his lifetime he amassed a most comprehensive collection of artefacts dating from the Stone Age, Iron Age and medieval period, right up until his own time. He had a wonderful insignia of the Irish Volunteers of 1782. His collection was so rare and interesting that part of it was loaned to the Irish Exhibition and Chicago Exhibition. Robert Day died at his residence, Myrtle Hill House, Cork, on the 10 July 1914 at the ripe old age of seventy-nine.

Messrs Gurr, Johns & Company, auctioneers, in conjunction with the Cork firm of Marsh & Sons, organised the auction of the Robert Day collection. Because of the sheer scale of the number of items involved, the sale took place over a period of five days from 7 September to 11 September 1915. The auction catalogue was printed by the local firm of Guy & Co. and cost 2s 6d. An enormous 1,472 lots were to be sold at his former residence at Myrtle Hill House. A brief summary of the categories were as follows: porcelain, pottery, fine old silver, historical objects, ancient Irish amber and glass beads and finally his collection of rare books and pamphlets. Such was the quality of these antiquities that many prominent English buyers and institutions, such as the National Museum, travelled to Cork to bid for these precious objects.

From the very beginning of the auction, substantial prices were achieved as rival bidders outbid their opponents in a battle for their favourite pieces. The most interesting item of Cork furniture to be sold was a massive mirror in a carved frame

By Order of the Executors.   Catalogues 2/6 each.

WITHOUT RESERVE.

MYRTLE HILL HOUSE, CORK.

Catalogue of the Collection

. . OF . .

The Late ROBERT DAY, Esq., F.S.A.

(BOOK PLATE, ROBERT DAY, F.S.A., M.R.I.A.)

:: TO BE SOLD BY AUCTION, ::
SEPT. 7th, 8th, 9th, 10th, 11th, 1915.

Auctioneers :
GURR. JOHNS & CO. Ltd.,
1, King Street, St. James's, London.

CORK : PRINTED BY GUY & CO. LTD.

with the arms and motto of the city of Cork. This mirror was formerly in the old mayoralty house (now the Mercy Hospital) and was made by Francis Booker, Dublin, in 1737. Because of its strong Cork connection this mirror drew a lot of attention from local buyers and it eventually sold for £39.

It was the chance of a lifetime for serious collectors to acquire some of the rarest artefacts ever to come on to the market. But unfortunately, within seven short days, one of the finest collections ever amassed by a single individual was dispersed and absorbed into smaller private collections. Robert Day had achieved what no other Cork antiquarian had accomplished – his interest, knowledge and wealth resulted in a collection of the most complex, rare and interesting artefacts. His legacy lives on in his collection of glass lantern slides which survived and were later added to and extended by his son Alec Day, who was a *tour de force* in forming the Cork Camera Club in 1923.

Founder of Roches Stores

William Roche was born in 1874 near Killavullen in County Cork and came from a farming back-ground. He received only a rudimentary education, as it was common practice for children at this time, especially males, to be sent out to work to help support the rest of the family. The Roche family contacts in Cork City made the necessary arrangements so that William would be apprenticed to the drapery trade. Apprentices literally became little more than slaves to the large department stores of the late nineteenth century. They worked long, hard, arduous hours, lived in cramped conditions and were treated appallingly by their masters. Many of these boys and girls did not live to finish their apprenticeships due to poor diet, lack of proper sanitary facilities and being confined in a polluted atmosphere over long periods.

William spent his time with the well-known firm of Cash & Co. and after five years he decided to leave, despite not having completed his seven years' apprenticeship. He was ambitious and he decided that he would set up a business of his own. Being naïve and trusting, he was apparently swindled out of his money in his first two endeavours. With few options left, he borrowed £70 from his parents, which they could ill afford to lose. Fortunately, his new enterprise, a small retail shop, broke even, so he was able to repay the loan by selling the business.

William then decided to head for the vast metropolis of London to make his fortune. Upon his arrival, he discovered that there was no work to be had for a young Irishman and London was an unforgiving place to survive in alone. The little money he had was rapidly running out, but he finally he got a job paying £40 per year. He had to work a fourteen-hour day, and on Saturdays the hours were extended to fifteen and a half. Eventually he left this job for a better one and gradually, through hard work, he saved £225 – enough to start a small business.

In 1900 he returned to Cork and opened a household and furniture shop in a side street at No. 22 Merchant Street (now part of Merchant's Quay shopping centre). Formerly known as Fish Street it housed only warehouses, sawmills and coal stores. To increase trade and storage William sold a share of his business to his friend, James Keating. They worked night and day so that their business would succeed, selling furniture, carpets, bedsteads, linoleum, etc. The premises had been converted and had a vast range of stock covering 12,320 square feet. They decided to sell ladies fashion from the premises, an idea that was considered ridiculous at the time. Merchant Street was an unfashionable side street near Merchant's quay, where ships and prostitutes plied their trade, and it was scandalous to suggest that ladies would frequent such an area. But bargains were to be had and citizens of Cork have always had an eye for good value, so his venture succeeded.

By the early 1900s, the partners had produced a lavish catalogue consisting of one hundred and eighty pages. It was distributed in both the city and county at enormous expense. Every order and letter sent to the business was personally seen to by one of the partners. The rapid success of their Cork Furniture Stores meant that it soon occupied building Nos 12, 13, 19, 22, 30, 31, 32 and 33 Merchant Street. The prosperity of the business was mainly due to extremely low overheads enabling them to sell goods at least 25 per cent cheaper than their rivals. The large department stores of Cash & Co., The Munster Arcade and The Queen's Old Castle, to name but a few, had huge

A SIDE STREET ·

overheads. The combination of large heating and light bills, directors' fees, managers' salaries, buyers' and assistants' wages made them less competitive.

An example of the good value offered is illustrated by a letter written to the firm by M. Carmody of Belgooly, Kinsale, dated 5 August 1902 and reprinted in their trade catalogue:

> Dear Sirs,
> I am highly pleased with the furniture that you have supplied me and am thoroughly convinced of the fact that I could not

get better value elsewhere. I have seen articles somewhat similar in appearance to those I purchased from you, although they seemed if anything inferior in quality, they cost 30 per cent more than your prices. I would recommend all who want to get real value for their money in the furniture line to deal with the Cork Furniture Stores and help to stem the tide of emigration by supporting home industries.

Wishing your business every success,

I remain,

Yours Sincerely,

M. Carmody.

Further expansion followed with the purchase of London House at No. 15 Patrick Street in 1919. The premises was renamed Roches Stores Ltd, and the business survived and flourished for a little over one hundred years.

The continual worry of operating a business with military curfews, raids, looting, shootings and the general harassment of citizens was taking its toll on trade during the fight for Irish freedom in the 1920s. London House was burned to the ground on the night of 11 December 1920 by British military forces, with the rest of the city centre. Fortunately some precautions had been taken and much of the stock at nearby warehouses was saved. These salvaged goods were put on sale in the old store and within a week turnover had doubled. Roches Stores continued for many years operating from temporary premises until the new building on Patrick's Street was completed in January 1927. The cost of this new modern department store was £26,474 16s 10d.

William Roche died on 23 February 1939, at the age of sixty-five, having achieved his aim of founding a reputable Cork firm, Roches Stores.

Arson and Murder

A s early as 9 October 1920, attempts had been made to deliberately set fire to Cork City Hall and a fireman was on constant duty there until its final destruction in December 1920. Bombs had been thrown through the windows from the Albert Quay side and the windows were boarded up to prevent missiles entering the building. Indeed it came as no surprise to the citizens of Cork that plans were afoot by the British military authorities to burn more buildings in an attempt to terrorise republican forces into submission.

Following a successful republican ambush at Dillon's Cross, crown forces were in a foul mood. Now came their opportunity to wreak havoc on the centre of Cork City. But first, known republican sympathisers had to be dealt with. The home of Cornelius and Jeremiah Delaney, members of the Irish Volunteers, was raided and both brothers were shot. Jeremiah died instantly and Cornelius died from his wounds a week later. Eye-witness accounts stated that the perpetrators of these crimes spoke with English accents and wore military uniforms.

The city was next in line for evil deeds and revenge was planned for the night of 11 December 1920. Members of the British Labour Commission, staying in Cork before the destruction, stated in their report that they were struck by the sense of impending disaster which appeared to hang over the city before that night. This tension had been further intensified by General Tom Barry's successful ambush at Kilmichael. This military engagement inflicted heavy casualties on British forces, which had appeared invincible up to then. The Dillon's Cross ambush was not the direct catalyst for destroying the commercial heart of the city, but the ambush gave the British an excuse to cause the devastation of Cork City.

The military curfew imposed on the city between the hours of 10 p.m. and 3 a.m. forbade Cork citizens to be out of doors without official military permission. At 9 p.m., just before curfew, the British military started to fire indiscriminately at civilians, thereby clearing all the principal streets in the city. Fires began in several locations in Patrick Street and at 3 a.m. the City Hall was ablaze. Trucks filled with Black and Tans, intent on looting and destruction, patrolled the deserted burning streets. Petrol and explosives, which had been stockpiled, were whisked into lorries and brought to the city centre.

At 10.30 p.m. the first official call to the Cork City Fire Brigade was received – the department store of Grant & Co. on Patrick Street was on fire. The premises were initially saved by the speedy response of the fire brigade, but worse was to follow. The Munster Arcade and Cash & Co. had been set ablaze and there was no hope of saving either. The fire hoses were bayoneted by the military and firemen were fired upon, enabling the conflagration to take hold. On the opposite side of the river, Cork City Hall and the Carnegie Library on Anglesea Street were burning furiously with no hope of saving either.

The following morning the smouldering city, or what was left of it, resembled a scene of destruction as bad as any that had been inflicted on any Belgian city after a German artillery bombardment during the First World War. The city had been destroyed by the people employed to protect it. The cover-up that followed defied all rational logic, with the British authorities blaming Sinn Féin extremists for the devastation. Chief Secretary of Ireland, Sir Hamar Greenwood and his cronies forged a map of Cork placing the City Hall in the city centre. An airborne spark had conveniently crossed the river from City Hall and incinerated the commercial heart of the city. The British policy of denial and blame went as far as maintaining that the crown forces had saved the remainder of the city. In the House of Commons Lieutenant Commander Kenworthy, a Liberal Member of Parliament, asked Greenwood if two civilians had been killed and if fire hoses had been cut by bayonets. Greenwood replied: 'There is not one atom of evidence that I know of to that effect.' Apparently the cover-up concluded that neither an ounce of ammunition nor a gallon of petrol was unaccounted for by any of the Cork-based British military institutions.

An impartial inquiry was called for, with the Sinn Féin leaders and unionists throwing their full political weight behind this demand. An enormous amount of valuable property was mysteriously destroyed, thousands of people were left unemployed, hundreds were made homeless and the citizens were left in a state of fear. The British government fearing the results of such an inquiry, conducted their own military investigation. The results of this two-day sham, where the perpetrators were also the judge and jury, were never published. It was estimated that the damage to property amounted to $20,000,000. There were six hundred and two claims for compensation; The Munster Arcade was the first case to be heard, and the sum of £405,000 was claimed for damages. The court decided that the amount claimed was exaggerated and having heard evidence awarded the reduced sum of £213,647.

William Roche claimed compensation for his shop, London House. Amongst the items he claimed compensation for was a Union Jack flag which was consumed in the inferno. He believed that his case was treated more sensitively because the court believed he had unionist sympathies.

It took many years for the city to recover from this tragedy, with many shops operating from temporary wooden structures. Cork was without an official City Hall until the construction of the present building in 1934, but Rebel Cork rose phoenix-like from the ashes as it had so many times before in its long turbulent history.

The City Flooded

The great frost of 1739 was one the most severe ever experienced in the annals of Cork history. In December of that year the River Lee had frozen so hard that it had become a huge block of ice. Tents were erected from the North Strand (east of present-day MacCurtain Street) all the way towards Blackrock Castle and Cork's citizens were not slow to enjoy the novelty of the amusements available on that occasion. Several days passed before the river began to thaw out and one day an adventurous gentleman, a Quaker, ventured too far on the thin ice which collapsed under his weight and he fell helplessly into the icy cold water. A local wit ran to the nearest tent and informed the owner that a Customs and Excise man had gone in under the water searching for smuggled goods.

Over eighty years passed before Cork experienced weather conditions as severe again. The year 1820 was recorded as having one of the most severe winters ever experienced, with everyone complaining bitterly about the cold weather – it was believed to be even more severe than the great frost of 1739. The River Lee was frozen solid and sledgehammers were used to break holes in the ice to enable farmers to get water for their livestock. The ice was so thick that people could cross the river at various places without the fear of falling in. On 17 January, as the ice began to thaw, heavy showers of sleet followed. Heavy falls of snow and bitterly cold winds blowing from the north-east came the next day. As night fell, violent showers of sleet and rain fell which caused the snow to melt and turn to slush again.

During the night the rain stopped, temperatures plummeted and another severe frost set in. Cork citizens found it very dangerous to even attempt to travel, making trading between towns and cities impossible. The extreme weather conditions lasted for five weeks and it was the poor people that were most affected by the dreadful circumstances prevailing. Many families were forced to sell their most basic possessions, even the very bedclothes on their beds were pawned, to put food on the table. The snow was several feet deep in the streets and in parts of the county the roads became impassable. A poor woman, overcome by the cold, collapsed to the ground and was covered by a large heap of snow near Gallows Green (Greenmount) – she was found there, frozen to death, the following morning.

The cold weather suddenly turned mild and it began to rain incessantly for two full days. Instead of conditions improving Cork citizens were faced with a new threat as the rain dissolved the mass of snow and ice on the high ground. The River Lee, from its source at Gougane Barra and all the tributaries feeding it, became a massive torrent of water and by 7 p.m. the city centre was engulfed by a flood of water the likes of which had never been seen before in living memory. Areas such as Cross Street, Nile Street, Hanover Street, Clarke's Marsh and Hammond's Marsh and the adjoining laneways were totally water-logged. Pieces of furniture, tables, chairs and other household belongings were seen floating in the flood waters.

The water engulfed houses, entering the windows and doors, destroying the contents. The occupants were forced to take refuge on the upper floors to escape drowning. Boats navigated up and down the streets which had become waterways and they were the only means of rescuing those poor wretches from drowning. Fortunately by dusk the water had receded, but even the ships moored on the main channels of the river were not safe. At 1 o'clock, a Welsh ship moored at Pope's Quay broke free from its moorings, and was swept away by the severe current. The captain and crew feared that they would be smashed against Patrick's Bridge so they decided to abandon ship.

A small boat was lowered into the turbulent water and the captain and two crew members jumped into it hoping to escape. But the boat became swamped by the choppy water and the captain and two crew members quickly drowned. The current carried the boat onwards and it soon became lodged in an arch of Patrick's Bridge. A further rescue attempt was not an easy task considering the prevailing conditions, but fortunately the remaining crew were saved due to the exertions of their heroic rescuers.

Controversial Election

The Cork election of 1852 was just like previous elections held in the city – controversy was not too far away. Claims, allegations and counter-claims were made on behalf of the various candidates and their election agents upon hearing the winning result. Due to the serious nature of the allegations presented to the authorities, a special commission was formed to investigate any impropriety. The select committee, under the auspices of Sir John Yarde Buller, investigated whether the winners, Francis Stack Murphy and William Fagan, were legally entitled to serve as parliamentary representatives for Cork. Colonel Chatterton and Mr Perrier were the two losing opposition candidates.

The election results were as follows: Murphy 1,246 votes, Fagan 1,220, Chatterton 898 and Perrier 194. Evidence was heard on behalf of the losing candidates, Chatterton and Perrier. Henry Fitzsimons, a solicitor and election agent, gave testimony on behalf of Colonel Chatterton, and testified about slanderous placards erected in various parts of the city. These notices claimed that outrages were committed on Catholic chapels, priests and nuns as a result of Chatterton's actions in parliament. It was also alleged that Catholic priests within the city supported these allegations and encouraged their congregations to vote for the opposing candidates, Murphy and Fagan.

Large crowds roamed the streets of the city and at Paul Street a mob attacked the house of a man named Mayne who had voted for Chatterton (at the time voting was not held in secret). Every pane of glass in his house was broken as he cowered under the stairs. On the north side of the city there was another gathering at the Shandon market polling booth. It was estimated that 3,000 men, armed with sticks, called for Chatterton's agent, Mr Bible, to come out. When Mr Bible failed to appear the shouting increased and the mob threatened to cut his guts out. Nearby a man named William Connor was rescued from the mob by a company of dragoons and brought to safety. It was recorded that the rioting and intimidation was the worst witnessed in over twenty years of controversial Cork elections.

Questions were also raised about the Custom House Ward and if the old theatre belonging to Mr Morrogh in Harpur's Lane was a suitable premises to use as a polling booth. It was also asserted that this was a neighbourhood where prostitutes plied their age-old trade. This evidence was vehemently denied, as the lane was located near the commercial heart of the city, namely off Paul Street.

Weeks before the election Jeremiah Murphy, a worker at MacSwiney's mill, promised his vote to Chatterton. His employer, Mr MacSwiney, upon hearing this dismissed him immediately. William Fagan promised that he would have him reinstated if he voted for him, but it appears he never returned to work at the mill again.

Another incident involved Daniel Desmond, a forty-two year old bricklayer and publican, whose business was located in Military Road. Desmond was approached by two priests, Father Scannell and Father Brown, requesting him to vote for Fagan. He said he could not as he had promised his vote to Chatterton. Father Brown, and some of his supporters, threatened that in a few short months 'he would not have a head to wear a hat'. The day of the election Desmond cast his vote in Chatterton's favour and at six o'clock in the evening his house was attacked. Every window, door and stick of furniture in the house was broken. Desmond tried to defend his home but a stone thrown by a Peg Casey struck him. He fell to the ground and was dealt several blows by a shoemaker by the name of Wall. Fortunately some soldiers dragged him to safety and bandaged his head wound at the barracks.

The soldiers did not escape injury from the mobs which patrolled the city, who often outnumbered them. Stones and missiles thrown by the crowds damaged the arms and accoutrements of the soldiers. The sum of £2 19s 3d was claimed as court expenses by witnesses from the civil authorities at Cork. The war office paid these expenses. No claim was made by the military from Cork Corporation for damages to rifles or military equipment.

The commission came to the following conclusion:

That the evidence adduced before the committee shows that, during the last election for ... Cork, riotous and tumultuous proceedings took place in the said city, and that serious outrages and assaults were committed on the persons and property of several electors and others.

It also found that intimidation and threats were made on several voters with the aim of controlling their votes. Meat, drink, refreshment and entertainment were also provided by the candidates, contrary to election policy, but no conclusive evidence was brought forward to link Murphy or Fagan with providing food or entertainment. Because of the ambiguous evidence, Francis Stack Murphy and William Fagan were declared elected for Cork.

Cork's Finest Hour

On 8 March 1901, a public meeting was held in Cork City Hall, where it was proposed to organise a major exhibition. This project was to rival the Cork exhibitions of 1852 and 1883 by its sheer size and scale. The Lord Mayor, Edward Fitzgerald, was the brain behind this ambitious idea. The initial plan was to house the exhibition at the rear of the municipal buildings on the site of the former 1883 exhibition, but the available space was totally inadequate. Various committees were formed to organise the event and money was to be collected in the form of subscriptions. Donations came from all over Ireland and Britain and in a short space of time £80,000 was raised to fund this novel venture.

A site was located on the land now known as Fitzgerald's Park situated opposite the gardens of Cork's more opulent citizens at Sunday's Well. The total area occupied over forty acres of landscaped gardens and the buildings towered over this scene. The Industry Hall was the largest building constructed, covering a massive 170,000 feet. Adjoining it was the Machinery Hall at two hundred by one hundred feet. The Concert Hall, a very important venue, could accommodate 2,000 people comfortably. This building housed a great organ, which was the largest such instrument in the south of Ireland. It was built by the local firm of T.W. Magahy at a cost of £1,200 and was later transferred to City Hall, but unfortunately British forces destroyed it when they burned City Hall in December 1920.

The exhibition was formally opened on 1 May 1902 by the Earl of Bandon and the Lord Mayor, Edward Fitzgerald. A vast procession comprising the various trades, with banners and bands, the lord mayors of Dublin and Belfast, the mayors of Derry, Waterford and Limerick (including the official mace and sword-bearers) made their way through the highly decorated streets of the city to the opening ceremony on the Mardyke. Golden keys were presented to the Earl of Bandon and the Lord Mayor, with which they opened the various buildings and these were soon filled to capacity. The entertainment consisted of a concert performed by an orchestra of four hundred musicians and singers. Notables such as Prince Henry of Prussia, the Duke of Connaught and the Lord Lieutenant Earl Cadogan and Countess Cadogan with the vice-regal party visited the exhibition.

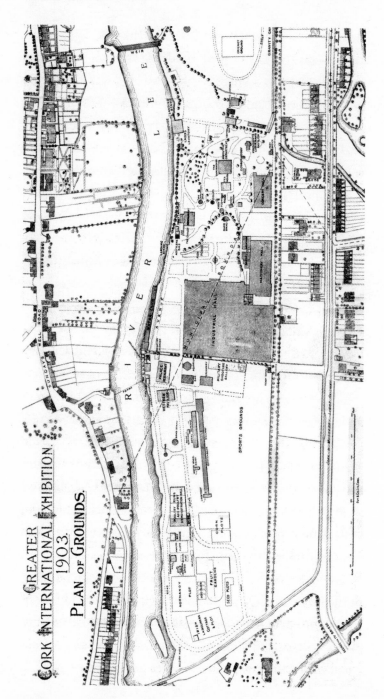

The entertainments were second to none and on the river, electric launches, gondolas and other vessels viewed the grand spectacle, floating lazily in the sunshine. One of the main attractions was the Great Water Chute, located close to the Industry Hall – it was seventy feet high. Passengers were carried up a gradual ascent to the summit, then went into the boats which were released down the chute, gaining impetus until with a sudden swoop they skimmed onto the water below. Another popular amusement was the switchback railway, an early form of roller-coaster and the first of its kind in Ireland. The latest technology was used, by adding a kick to the engine making it surge forward powerfully, which made it all the more exciting. An advertisement claimed, 'As a nerve tonic, a tour there and back on the switchback may be recommended.'

The women's section was entered through the grand entrance with its most interesting decorative architecture, comprising two doorways of Celtic design. These were exact reproductions of the doorways of Cormac's Chapel at Cashel and were made from fibrous plaster coloured to imitate old stone work. There were examples of almost every kind of handicraft work by women: tweeds, flannels, hosiery, fine lace work and embroidery were on display. Recent advances in the scientific world were demonstrated in the form of wireless telegraphic equipment, machinery for the production of liquid gases, and a complete X-ray plant. A wonder of the scientific world, radium, a new metal with remarkable qualities, was on display.

The agricultural section was represented with a working model of an Irish labourer's cottage on a half acre of land. A magnificent section was allocated to bee-keeping and poultry under the supervision of Messrs Hogg and Robertson. The fisheries section consisted of large tanks where specimens of trout, pike, perch, rudd, carp and eels could be observed. Fishing appliances such as boats, nets, lobster and crab pots and a complete range of artificial flies suitable for every district of Ireland were on display. At the entrance to the west gardens, five camels and three elephants were used to bring children from one end of the exotic gardens to the next. A canal was created to carry passengers in boats the two hundred yards from the entrance to the grounds proper. These boats ferried eight people per journey and took just sixty seconds from the ticket office.

From the opening day to 1 November 1902, a staggering one and a half million people paid admission to the grounds. The success of the exhibition led for calls to reopen it for the 1903 season and in May 1903 the Greater Cork International Exhibition was declared open to the public. King Edward and Queen Alexandra of Great Britain attended amidst great pomp and ceremony, much to the delight of the local aristocracy and public officials. The 1902–1903 Cork Exhibition was a resounding success and has not been equalled to this day.

Legend and Land Squabbles

A short distance from Cork City there is a lough which was formerly known as Lough na Fanog, or lake of the ferns. The water is provided by a complicated series of underground streams. The lough is an area of natural beauty and is an important bird sanctuary which is home to swans, geese and different species of duck. Crofton Croker wrote a wonderful account of the legend of the lough that told how there existed near Cork a mighty king called Corc, whose palace stood where the lough now is. In the middle of the courtyard there was a spring of water which was so pure and clear that it was a great wonder. People travelled from miles around to sample this precious water. The king, fearing the spring would run dry, built a high wall around it. His daughter Fioruisge was the only person with a key to enter.

One night the king gave a banquet and invited all the princes, lords and nobles to attend. One young prince had his eye on Fioruisge and he danced all night with her. Towards the end of the night one of the great lords requested some water and the king sent his daughter with a golden vessel to get some. The young prince accompanied her to the spring, and as she unlocked the door and stooped down with the vessel she lost her balance and fell in. The water rose so fast that the entire courtyard became flooded quickly. The water rose to such a height that the green valley was enveloped in water and so the Lough was formed. Although the king and his subjects were covered by the water, they were not drowned. His daughter, Fioruisge, returned safely to the banqueting hall.

It is said that the entertainment and dancing continues at the bottom of the lough and the only way to break the spell is to recover the golden vessel and bring it above the water. When the waters of the lough are low and clear, the tops of the towers can be clearly seen. This legend was first published in Crofton Croker's *Fairy Legends and traditions of the South of Ireland* in 1824. Older legends existed describing this lough as 'where the pool now standeth there lived vicious and beastlie inhabitants'.

As early as 1695 the corporation of Cork ordered that Alderman Wright, Mr Rogers and Mr Champion survey some ground near the lough with a view to valuing and renting it. But the lough proved to be a troublesome issue for the corporation. In October 1717, Will Masters was ordered to give up his lease on land near the lough under threat of legal action, but he refused to do so. Eight years later the legal wrangling continued and the sum of £7 18*s* was offered to Masters upon his surrendering the lease, the legal costs fixed at 30*s*. By 1727, trespassing had become a vexatious issue and representatives of the corporation were sent to the lough to issue a report and deal with the offenders. Richard Caulfield's *Council Book* records that for all the cattle that grazed on or about this land: 'in order to cool for slaughtering [their owners] shall pay one penny for every head and a halfpenny for every pig or sheep'.

The issue of having two fairs near the lough was examined as early as 1733. In later years it was recommended that three fairs be held which would generate much needed revenue for the city. In 1743, it was discovered that the lough had been over-fished and to conserve the remaining fish stocks it was ordered that 'no person shall fish with any net or nets in said Lough'.

The contentious issue of people digging up the ground and carrying away enormous amounts of soil, which was exceptionally rich due to its proximity to the lough, concerned the corporation for many more years. Even members of the Established Church had their eyes on this important piece of land and in 1770 Dean Chinnery built a wall and enclosed ground near the lough not belonging to him. He then offered to take a lease on the plot of land – the outcome of this incident is not recorded.

The lough was not just a place of commerce but of amusement as well. When it froze there was no place to equal it for sport in Cork. On 2 January 1767, the frost was so severe that the lough was frozen solid and skating became a popular pastime. It was so cold that many tradesmen could not work and because they had nothing better to do went to the lough and amused themselves by skating. Two weeks later the roads became impassable, as the snow was seven or eight feet deep in parts.

A century later there were many newspaper accounts of skating on the lough, including some of near tragedies when the ice broke and the skaters were hurled into the icy lake. There were many injuries: broken limbs and severe bruising were the order of the day. Many of the local hospitals had more than their fair share of ice-skating casualties.

The lough continues to be a safe haven for humans, animals and birds alike, a tranquil oasis not far from the hustle and bustle of the city centre.

Travelling in Cork

Jacques Louis de Latocnaye was a Breton who came from an aristocratic family and he had made his escape from France before the advent of the French revolution. He travelled extensively in Britain and Scotland and wrote a book about his adventures. Following the success of his book, he decided to travel to Ireland in 1795. He spent over eight months recording his observations for this book which was published in French. In 1798, M. Harris, whose printing establishment was located at No. 6 Castle Street, published an English version in two volumes. The title of this English translation was *Rambles through Ireland by a French Emigrant*. The book was dedicated to the Earl of Conyngham whose uncle, Burton Conyngham, sponsored the author on his travels in Ireland.

De Latocnaye set sail for Ireland from Milford Haven, which he described as an ugly hole where a traveller would spend every penny that he carried waiting for a fair wind. The price of the voyage was a guinea and a half, an exorbitant amount at that time. The ship made good progress and landed at Dublin, with a crossing time of twenty-four hours. Upon landing he discovered much to his dismay that the revenue commissioners had levied a tax of 2*s* 6*d* on every passenger and their luggage. His first encounter with a carriage driver made him swear, as the driver stopped at every ale house on their route for a drink. The driver said to his friends: 'I am sure he is a jointleman for he swears confoundedly.' Although obviously an educated man of some class, as a foreigner he readily mixed with, and would appear to have been accepted by, all classes of Irish society.

Upon his arrival in Cork he noted the complete lack of clean water available to the poorer classes who collected water that fell from the roofs of houses or in the nearby channel of the River Lee. The streets were extremely dirty and both the North and South Main Streets had prisons at either end. These, he believed, prevented the free circulation of air into the city due to their elevated positions and the stench emanating from them. He observed that hideous-looking beggars had taken control of the side wall at the Cornmarket and were begging for food of any description. Begging was the only option for many women, especially if their husband died, as the poor widow had to go begging to survive. But nothing could persuade the people to send their children to the Foundling Hospital, where they would be educated in the Protestant religion, never again to see their parents.

A great number of characters existed in Cork at the time, many with strange notions. One such individual could not stand the smell of meat in the kitchen, so he ended up eating alone in the hallway of his house. Another captivated his audience with his beautiful voice and charming music, but unexpectedly became violent and attacked without warning. One Cork character who was quite mad believed that there was a conspiracy to poison him and when a person bought bread at the baker's shop he quickly snatched it as he believed that it was safe to eat since it was not meant for him. He did the same thing in the butcher's shop and every other premises he entered.

Latocnaye next visited the Protestant bishop and when he presented a letter of recommendation he was treated very well. There appeared to be no religious antagonism between the two main religions and he was sent by his host to see Dr Moylan the Catholic bishop, a well respected and educated man.

Latocnaye made some suggestions concerning the state and location of the two prisons, which gave him some cause for concern, recommending that they be pulled down. He also proposed that the streets be cleaned, the pigs removed from them, the rebuilding of the Cornmarket in a more suitable place, the demolition of the ruined houses on the quays, construction of schools, and fountains to be provided for the public. If this were achieved, our traveller believed, Cork would match Dublin in fifty years because of the ideal location of the port to expand and export its produce. The exporting of meat was one of the main trades in the city and one merchant boasted that he killed between 20–25,000 pigs annually.

De Latocnaye, the intrepid traveller, said goodbye to his friends and the good people of Cork City and headed in the direction of Bandon.

A rare panoramic stereo view of Cork city taken from Audley Place in the 1860s

Engraving commemorating the rescue of passengers from the rock near
the wreck of the paddle steamer *Killarney*, 1838

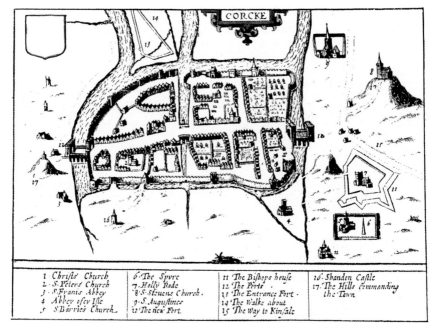

1 *Chrifts Church*	6 *The Spyre*	11 *The Bifhops houfe*	16 *Shandon Caftle*
2 *S Peters Church*	7 *Holly Rode*	12 *The Ports*	17 *The Hills commanding*
3 *S Franis Abbey*	8 *S Steuens Church*	13 *The Entrance Fort*	*the Town*
4 *Abbey ofev Ifle*	9 *S Augustines*	14 *The Walke about*	
5 *S Barries Church*	10 *The new Fort*	15 *The Way to Kinfale*	

John Speede's map of Corcke, 1610

Sections from Charles Smith's prospect of Cork, 1750

Early commercial postcard view of the Cork & Muskerry train on the
Western Road

Early animated postcard warning Corkonians of the danger of
electric trams, 1898

Early stereo view showing the remains of Kilcrea Abbey, burial place of Art Ó Laoighre

Engraving from 1774 of the old Exchange building which was situated at Castle Street, Cork

Sir Edward
Fitzgerald, Lord
Mayor of Cork,
1901–3

Devastation of the heart of the city centre following the looting and
burning of Cork by British forces in December 1920

John Fitzgerald, the famous
Cork poet known as the
Bard of the Lee

The 1902/3 Cork Exhibition water chute in action

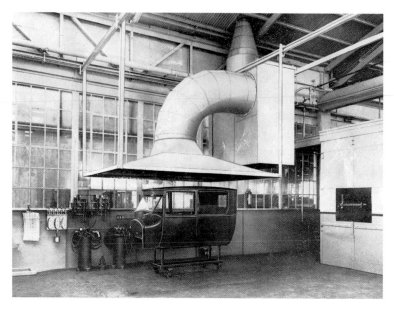

The latest technology at Ford's paint department, 1926

Awaiting delivery – the finished products outside the Ford plant, 1926

Engraving showing St Patrick's Bridge and some of Cork's principal churches, *c.* 1870

Stereo view from 1877 of Shandon church, graveyard and the Green Coat School

Early view of South Gate Bridge and prison

The *Cork Advertiser and Commercial Register* for 18 June 1799 advertising Irish lottery tickets

☞ LOSE NO TIME.

27 Capital Prizes

Are in the IRISH LOTTERY to be drawn on 23d July next,

THE TICKETS AND SHARES

Of which are now on Sale at the

Old Hibernian Office,

NO. 12, CAPEL-STREET, DUBLIN.

The Character the above Office has maintained for 19 Years will, BROWNE presumes, establish for his SHARES a decided preference.

TICKET BUYERS

in the City of Cork, and its Vicinity, are respectfully acquainted that TICKETS and SHARES, from BROWNE's Office, can be had at

MR. JAMES HALY's,

KING'S-ARMS, EXCHANGE, CORK,

At the most reduced Prices.

TO BE SOLD BY AUCTION,

CORNELIUS LEHANE, OF CORK, IRELAND

NOTED ORATOR AND LABOR LEADER

Organizer of the Wolfe Tone Literary Society in Ireland.
Leader of the Great Gas Workers Strike in Cork, Ireland.
Organizer of the Socialist Party of Great Britain.
Organizer of the Warehousemen and Clerks Union of Great Britain.
Founder and Editor of the "London Socialist Standard".
Cartoonist on the "Cork Examiner".
Delegate to the Irish Trades Union Congress

Will deliver an address on

"Ireland, England and the European War"

Union Hall, Main St., Madison, Maine

MONDAY EVE., JAN. 25, 1915, 8 o'clock

ADMISSION, 10 CENTS

Everybody Invited—Do Not Miss This—The Treat of a Lifetime

Cornelius Lehane, leader of the Cork Gas Worker's strike, 1915

Denis Lenihan (author's father) on a Murphy's horse and dray, 1956

Old commercial view of the Mercy Hospital, formerly the mayor's residence, *c.*1900

Early stereo view of tall ships on Cork's quays in the 1870s

Right: The old cathedral church of St Finbarr's prior to its demolition

Below: Its replacement, the magnificent French Gothic cathedral by Burges

Republican Lord Mayor Tomás MacCurtain, murdered in front of his wife and family by British forces

Republican Lord Mayor Terence MacSwiney, who died on hunger strike for his beliefs

The old reading
room of the Cork
Commercial
Buildings, South Mall,
Cork, now part of the
Imperial Hotel

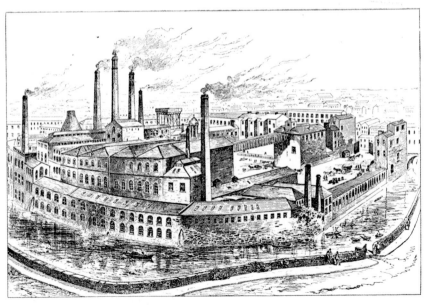

An industrious sketch of Beamish Brewery, South Main Street, in its
halcyon days, alas now consigned to memory

Industry coopers at work making barrels for Beamish stout

An iconic advertisement showing Eugene Sandow lifting a horse above his head promoting the benefits of drinking Murphy's stout

Catholic Bishop,
Protestant Landlord

John Butler was born in 1731, the third son of Edmond Butler, eighth Baron of Dunboyne. He came from an extremely wealthy family who owned immense tracts of land across the counties of Munster and Leinster. John was educated as a Catholic and at an early age chose the priesthood as his profession. His brothers, Pierce and Edmond, joined the army and went to fight in the war of the Austrian succession. John left for Rome to continue his studies at the Irish College. During his time there he lost his left eye as the result of a duel. In 1755, at the Basilica of St John Lateran, he was ordained a priest.

Three years later he successfully completed a doctorate of divinity and he decided to return to Ireland. He quickly rose through the ranks becoming a parish priest, an archdeacon, and a bishop's secretary. When the position of Bishop of Cork became vacant in 1763, his family connections and wealth ensured that he obtained the position.

Bishop Butler was very careful not to antagonise the Protestant establishment, as this was a crucial period when the Penal Laws were being relaxed against Catholics. He spoke out strongly against Whiteboy activity (membership of such organisations could result in excommunication) and the contentious issue of tithe-collecting by the Protestant clergy.

In 1786 his life changed when he inherited the title of eleventh Baron of Dunboyne by default, as both his brothers and his nephew had died, leaving him as the sole surviving male heir. His religion would not allow him to marry and he had taken the vow of celibacy, so it looked like the twelfth century baronetcy would die out. In December he took the bold step of resigning as Bishop of Cork after twenty-three years service and he petitioned the pope to relieve him of his vow of celibacy. In his letter he pleaded: 'It was no pleasure for me after a life of celibacy to share my bed and board.' The pope refused to grant this request. Butler had believed rather naively that his request would be granted because he had come from a noble bloodline.

In 1787, he sacrificed everything so that he might produce an heir and converted to the Protestant religion, allowing him to marry a cousin, Maria Butler. This marriage produced a premature baby girl who died almost immediately. Butler, or as he was now known, Baron Dunboyne, was distraught, so he moved to Dublin with his wife hoping to keep out of the limelight.

In Cork the marriage was scandalous news – the Catholic Bishop of Cork had renounced his religion, married a cousin and become a protestant all in one fell swoop. The whole affair was unbelievable and unforgivable. He was denounced from every Cork pulpit and Rev. Arthur O'Leary published a pamphlet condemning him to hell. An anonymous contemporary satire went as follows:

Later when you are in hell
And your tears flow
That is when you discover
Which is better, a priest or minister.

Many instances exist where Butler showed his remorse, such as during the rebellion of 1798 when the little chapel at Dunboyne was destroyed. On hearing of its destruction he offered to have the chapel rebuilt, paid for from his own funds. Another story tells that he gave his own chalice, dated 1621, to the local priest near Fethard saying, 'Here is a chalice for you with which I often celebrated mass in happier days, take it from my polluted hands.' In 1800, Butler was sixty-nine years old in failing health and was trapped in an unhappy marriage. He wrote a letter of repentance to the pope regretting his actions and begging forgiveness. It appears that his request was granted as Father William Gahan heard his final confession and he reconverted to Catholicism on his deathbed. He died in Dublin and, in accordance with his wishes, he was buried in the Augustinian Friary at Fethard, Tipperary.

But the saga was not to end there. Butler had left a huge portion of his wealth and property to St Patrick's Maynooth but his relatives disputed the will. It was possible that under the terms of the Penal Laws the will could be declared null and void, leaving both parties with expensive legal bills. Litigation dragged on for several years before a compromise was reached between the college and the Butler family. In 1808 the great scandal of the Bishop of Cork which had rocked the Catholic Church to its foundations was finally over. John Butler, the one-eyed Catholic Bishop of Cork and Protestant Baron Dunboyne, had finally paid restitution for his sins. But he was only one of two members of the Irish Catholic hierarchy to become an apostate (a person who renounces their former religion), a position he holds to this day. The other being the notorious Miler McGrath of Cashel, the sixth Bishop of Down and Connor.

Eccentric Historian

Abraham Abell was born at Pope's Quay, Cork, on 11 April 1783. His father Richard was a prominent merchant in the city. His family were Quakers and had been practising their religion in Cork for nearly two hundred years. Abraham was successfully employed in the family business and became involved in all the main literary, scientific and charitable institutions of the period. He was a founder member of the Cork Scientific and Literary Society, the Cuverian Society, treasurer to the Cork Library, manager of the Cork Institution and managing director of the fledgling Cork Savings Bank. He was involved in many charitable societies and was treasurer of the Cork Dispensary and Humane Society. He always remained neutral in his political and religious beliefs and as a result he was held in high esteem.

Abraham had an extremely inquisitive mind and he turned his attention to the scientific study of magnetism and archaeology, in equal measure. He amassed a magnificent collection of ancient relics and coins, and a large library of rare and unusual books. Local residents saw him as an extremely eccentric character and some of his actions justified this impression. Once when travelling to Curabinny Hill near Cork Harbour, he became so excited upon discovering an ancient burial mound that he rolled down each side yelling loudly.

He lived very frugally and all his energies were spent in pursuit of his interests. He slept on a bare mattress with only his papers for a pillow. When he was young he had heard ghost stories which left an indelible impression on him. To conquer his fears and superstitions, he slept for several weeks between two skeletons, which, apart from being highly unusual, must have been extremely uncomfortable.

At the time the inhabitants of Cork did not view horse meat as an agreeable food, but when Abraham heard of the unexpected death of his father's young horse he decided that now was the time to try it. A fine cut of horse meat was put into a barrel of brine to season it and, having tasted this meat, he proclaimed that he had never enjoyed a meal so much in his whole life. Occasionally he fasted for a full twenty-four hours to reduce his weight, although he was not like his father who was quite overweight.

When he was working in his shop he would have a cat at each side and sometimes his favourite tom-cat sat on his shoulder purring all the while. Abraham would exclaim that it was like music and that the sound cheered him during his working day.

Abraham never married, although he was once in love, but the girl he loved died at a young age. When he retired from business, he decided he would like to spend the rest of his days living in the old medieval tower of the Red Abbey (near Douglas Street). When he went to inspect his chosen residence he discovered to his dismay that the tower had been converted into a great chimney. The nearby houses had diverted their chimney smoke through a series of flues into the tower covering the inside in black soot. This forced him to change his plans and he rented rooms in the Cork Institution (now part of the Crawford Gallery). He lived here as a recluse, with his books covering the walls and floors of his room. He often spent his time reading well into the night and he stood to prevent falling asleep. He reportedly went one step further on occasion, strapping his legs together thus enabling him to stand and read on longer through the night. Each year he celebrated his birthday by walking one mile for every year that he lived. Upon reaching the age of fifty-eight years, he walked all the way to Youghal and back.

At times Abraham was prone to fits of depression and in April 1848 he decided to abandon all of his interests. In a moment of insanity he gathered up all his books, papers and music and put them into a barrel and set them on fire, destroying his lifetime's work. He quickly realised the folly of his actions and immediately started collecting again.

He seldom answered letters, as he intensely disliked writing, although his friends hoped that he would leave behind some manuscripts of his studies. Unfortunately this never happened and Abraham Abell died on 12 February 1851 at sixty-eight years of age. He was one of Cork's zaniest characters leaving behind a legacy of science, antiquities and a large collection of 4,500 books.

Queen's Arson

The building of Queen's College Cork, now UCC, began in the first year of the famine, 1845. The building was completed in time for the opening ceremony on 7 November 1849. The leading architects of the day, Deane and Woodward, designed the college. The Deane family were responsible for some of the city's most notable buildings, including the Courthouse, St Mary's church on Pope's Quay and the Cork Savings Bank. The blueprint for the college did not follow Deane's usual classical style but was based on a gothic design influenced by Oxford College.

The inaugural address given by the president of Queen's College, Sir Richard Kane, degenerated into a total farce. The Italian professor of Trinity College, Signor Angeli, had been commissioned to translate a portion of Kane's speech into Italian. Unfortunately Angeli made such a blundering attempt, that it was widely believed that the translation was not Italian at all. Signor Angeli was quickly dismissed from his post at Trinity College.

Initially the campaign to found a college in Cork had been orchestrated by leading merchants within the city. they were united in this common cause in the late 1830s. But by 1859, Catholics and Protestants were at loggerheads about the control of the college. The Catholic clergy were demanding a greater say in the running of its affairs, whilst the Protestant side were against this, fearing a Catholic monopoly. The Catholic hierarchy used its influence within the city to stem the tide of Catholic graduates entering the college, in order to gain greater control of its administration. The squabbling of the professors and the president, who controlled every aspect of the college, led to mismanagement. The appointment to professorships of candidates whose qualifications were dubious, over more experienced individuals, did not promote its reputation. In 1859 local author Brian Cody recorded that:

> Advertising for candidates for a vacant chair in the Queen's College is of late a mere farce; and in looking for it, an able Irishman with the highest testimonials will have little or no chance against a mediocre Englishman or Scotsman who has never been previously heard of.

It was obvious that the college was not functioning properly as President Kane was absent more often than he was there, yet the government was pumping in £8,000 per year to keep it above water. These circumstances, allied with the bad feeling of Catholics incensed by their clergy, had disastrous consequences for the college. In the early morning of 15 May 1862 smoke and flames was seen coming from the roof and windows of the west wing of the college. By the time the fire brigade arrived, the fire was out of control and all the firemen could do was to contain it. The medical, engineering and agricultural departments suffered losses or were destroyed. Fortunately the library survived, as did the natural history museum, but the collection of classical casts was destroyed. Initial reports indicated that the fire was started deliberately but the question was, who had committed the dastardly deed?

A reward of £150 was offered to find the culprit, or indeed the culprits. No one was beyond suspicion, even the president was accused by Dr Bullen, one of the college professors. Dr Bullen had ambitions to become president himself, but he was removed from his position as professor

of surgery because of his allegations. A parliamentary commission was set up to find some answers but this commission provided more questions than answers. Everyone connected with the college was a suspect, as were half the city's Catholic inhabitants – all having a motive for setting fire to this ungodly establishment. The college porters became the main suspects for a time, until Catholic fanatics became the main scapegoats.

As time went by the conspiracy theories increased and the pathology laboratory became the focus of attention. Rumours circulated that it was deliberately set on fire to destroy crucial evidence in a forthcoming murder trial. Richard Burke, a clerk of the Waterford poor law union, was accused of poisoning his wife with arsenic, and it was believed that he was having an affair with another woman. Part of the dead woman's stomach had been sent to the pathology laboratory in the college for examination and the results would have been crucial to the prosecution's case.

The arsonists were never discovered although without doubt, according to the official government report, the fire was started deliberately. The question of compensation was also challenged by the rate-payers of the city as it was believed that a disgruntled employee could have started it. The fire of 1862 became part of local folklore and the mystery of who started it remains to this day.

Black Eagle of the North

John Murphy was born on 23 December 1796; he was the second son of James Murphy a wealthy Cork merchant and ship-owner. His father's business was extremely successful as he imported tea, sugar, pepper, coffee, Jamaican rum – in fact merchandise from all over the world was sold in his store. The relaxation of the Penal Laws enabled him to invest his money in property, although covertly, and as his wealth grew he purchased land and property in the city.

At an early age, John took an interest in his father's business. He listened intently to his father's stories of far-away lands and ships laden with exotic cargoes of fruit, spices and tea. As a little boy he longed to see the world and all it contained.

At the time it was normal practice for well-to-do Catholics to send their offspring to England or France to be educated. At the tender age of eight, John was sent across the sea to England to be taught privately. He set sail on the *Belay & Mary* which regularly called at the port of Cork. Having landed its cargo, it would return to Liverpool laden with butter, tallow and hides. Captain Rogers and his wife looked after young John throughout the voyage. When the ship docked at Liverpool on Sunday morning, he accompanied them to church. Upon discovering that it was a Protestant service, not a Catholic ceremony, John kicked up a terrible racket. His guardians were extremely embarrassed and were forced to leave the church because of his tantrums. Even at a young age he was a headstrong, stubborn individual with a mind of his own.

Upon leaving school in 1810, John returned to Cork to work in his father's business. After two years he was bored and he joined the East India Company. He enlisted as a midshipman aboard the *Charles Grant*, under the command of Captain John Locke. He spent almost two years on voyages to far-flung destinations, but in August 1814, he parted company with his ship. He invested his little fortune on risky investments, much to his father's despair. But soon wanderlust struck again and he set out to explore the world once more.

By July 1816, his travels brought him to Lake Superior, which was the main fur trading centre in North America. He joined the Hudson Bay Trading Company as a clerk, on a salary of thirty shillings per year. The company obtained furs from the native Americans at little cost, and resold them in England at enormous profit. John quickly became friendly with the natives and the Company, seeing the advantages of this friendship, made him chief clerk in charge of trading. As time went by, John spent more and more of his time in the native community, challenging their young braves to feats of strength and skill. The tribes respect for him grew with each passing day, until they considered him one of their own. Eventually he was honoured by the elders in an elaborate ceremony and given the title 'Black Eagle of the North'.

In 1822, he was on the move again and headed for

London on the Company's ship the *Eddystone*. He spent many years there in business until he decided to enter the English College in Rome to study for the priesthood. He was ordained in March 1844 and a month later he was assigned to the parish of Liverpool – a congested dockland area which was home to thousands of Irish immigrants. The two existing Catholic churches could not cope with the vast sea of humanity so he purchased All Saints, the old Protestant church, to cater for the expanding flock. With the onset of the famine, more and more people fled from Ireland to escape hunger and disease. He tended the sick and buried the dead until he himself became a victim of the famine fever.

He was sent to Cork to convalesce. Bishop Murphy, his uncle, had died in April 1847 and his successor Bishop Delaney called upon the enigmatic Father Murphy to travel to Goleen to combat a local Protestant landowner Fisher, who was feeding the hungry and giving them money to convert to Protestantism. Riding through the grounds of the Protestant church on his magnificent stallion, he implored the newly converted to return to their former religion. His mission was a resounding success and the reconverted Catholics publicly forsook the Protestant religion at Fisher's gate. Father Murphy spent vast sums of money from his own funds on food and clothing in an effort to relieve some of the misery in West Cork.

His next assignment was the rebuilding of a new church to replace Carey's Lane chapel in Cork City. A new parish church was needed to accommodate the ever-growing

inner-city population. Unfortunately the proposed site was extremely small and nearby land was not available. The foundation stone was laid on 15 August 1859. The architect Pugin designed the gothic church, which was considered by some to be a little too ornate. Collecting the necessary funding was an enormous task – even pennies from the poor were collected. One day, while canvassing with his sister, he called to a local undertaker. The undertaker was asked to subscribe to the rebuilding project, but he sarcastically refused, saying, 'you give me no business'. Without hesitation Father John requested that his sister and himself should be measured for two coffins. Immediately the undertaker responded and subscribed to the building fund.

Father John Murphy died on 10 March 1883. Stories of this legendary figure, whose career and exploits as a merchant, fur trader, honorary Indian and finally priest and church builder, are still told in the city of his birth.

Henry Ford

In November 1916 formal negotiations took place between Henry Ford & Son, Cork Corporation and the Harbour Commissioners. Ford offered to purchase the freehold of the Cork Park Racecourse and land adjoining the river. The proposed site was over one hundred and thirty-six acres. In January 1917, a special act of parliament was passed to enable the company to buy these lands and obtain permission to erect a large factory to manufacture tractors. Under this agreement Henry Ford & Son acquired the freehold and land which had a river frontage of 1,700 feet. The estimated cost of construction was £200,000 and the factory was to employ at least 2,000 male employees at the minimum rate of one shilling per hour.

The plant was specifically designed for the manufacture of agricultural tractors which were sold under the brand name Fordson. These tractors were driven by a twenty-two horse-power four-cylinder engine which was powered by kerosene or paraffin. These machines were extremely versatile as various attachments could be powered by attaching a drive belt to the engine. By that time the First World War was ending, but every available mechanical device was still geared to supplying the military machine. As food production was essential, horse-drawn machinery was no match for this new technology because the Fordson tractor could pull two fourteen-inch ploughs effortlessly, even in the toughest soil conditions. The location of the plant was a godsend for Cork, as no other industry could provide such employment or engineering dominance

Unfortunately the choice of site was not ideal, as it had to be levelled and piled, which delayed the building of the factory. When completed, the total floor area was a massive 330,000 square feet and production began in the summer of 1919. In an interview given to the *Los Angeles Examiner* Henry Ford gave this reason for choosing Cork:

> My ancestors came from near Cork and that city with its wonderful harbour has an abundance of fine industrial sites. We chose Ireland for a plant because we wanted to start Ireland on the road to industry. There was, it is true, some personal sentiment in it.

The wharf frontage was indeed ideal as ships brought the raw material right to the very doors of the factory. The finished tractors could be transferred all over the globe by the same shipping method.

In 1922 the Ford factory had its most charismatic visitor, when Michael Collins, chairman of the Provisional Government, arrived on a surprise visit. 'The quay workers immediately identified the distinguished visitor and cheers were raised all along the riverside.'

Gradually it became uneconomic to produce tractors as demand continued to fall and the decision to cease tractor production meant that Cork was to become an assembly plant only. But in 1929 Cork was once again refitted for tractor production due to the closure of their competitor Dearborn's tractor division. A massive order was received by Cork to supply parts to service the 25,000 tractors operating in Russia. By 1930 Cork was exporting tractors as far afield as China, Fiji and Malaysia.

In 1929, a bold initiative was introduced to make the transportation of coal from the supply ships moored at Ford's wharf more efficient. It was proposed to build a miniature railway on the roof of the building to carry the coal. A Lister petrol locomotive was purchased along with five transport wagons. The engine proved to be inadequate and Ford's engineers designed and built their own eight-horse-power engine. The ingenious plan involved filling a hopper, also located on the roof, with coal and transferring the coal from the hopper into the wagons. The locomotive then transported the coal to its desired location, where the bottom of the wagons opened, depositing the coal. This remarkable line was in operation for about eighteen years until its demise in 1950. Ford's was probably the only factory in Ireland to have its own private railway located on the roof of its production building.

Following the outbreak of the Second World War, the factory was brought to its knees due to the lack of available raw material or markets to sell to. Everything and anything was recycled: old tram axles were salvaged and remodelled, gun carriages were produced for the Irish army. There was also a shortage of screwdrivers and these were manufactured and supplied to Woolworths. Even old nails were straightened and timber was recycled from old packing crates for which the Ford employees were paid the princely sum of 9*d* per hour. By 1950, the company had sufficiently recovered to celebrate the building of 75,000 vehicles and were manufacturing 'Ireland's Most Popular Car', the Ford Prefect. Following the factory's fiftieth anniversary in 1967, £2,000,000 was spent on modernising the assembly plant.

On Friday 13 July, 1984, due to harsh economic conditions, the Cork factory closed, making over eight hundred workers redundant. Many Ford workers were never to find employment again; some had worked for over forty years at the Cork plant. It was indeed the end of an era.

Folklore of Cork

Thomas Crofton Croker was born at Buckingham Square, Cork, in 1798. In 1812, he was apprenticed to the Quaker merchants, Lecky and Mark, on Charlotte Quay and he showed a great talent for antiquarian research. At this time he became friendly with the antiquarian Abraham Abell and they shared literary and antiquarian interests with another fellow historian Joseph Humphries. In 1813, they travelled to Gougane Barra, where people went on pilgrimage. It was widely believed that the waters had curative properties where humans and animals could be cured of their ailments. Whilst mixing and drinking with the locals, they heard stories and singing in Irish, and this encounter with Irish music and language impressed Croker so much that he decided to learn more.

He first put pen to paper with a poem he translated from Irish and it was published in the *Morning Post*. He was also skilled at drawing and sketching. In 1817, he exhibited as an artist at the Munster Fine Arts exhibition which was held in Cork. Upon the death of his father in 1818, he took up a position in the British admiralty. Three years later he visited Ireland and this resulted in the publication of *Researches in the South of Ireland* in 1924. The full title gives us a better understanding of its contents, *Researches in the South of Ireland illustrative of the Scenery, Architectural Remains, and the Manners and Superstitions of the Peasantry.*

It also contains a private narrative of the rebellion of 1798. This volume was published in London by John Murray with seventeen illustrations and it sold well both in Ireland and Britain.

Croker continued to collect stories, legends and traditions of the country people and he travelled great distances on poor roads by horse and car to record them. In 1825, he published *Fairy Legends and Traditions of the South of Ireland*, the first collection of oral tales published in either Britain or Ireland. For the first time the many different kinds of fairies or flying spirits such as the Shefro, Cluricaune, Banshee, Merrow, Pouke and Dullahan were chronicled. It was widely believed by the poorer people of Ireland that these fairies had a special influence or control over their lives. The importance of this research into the oral tradition of the poorer country people cannot be underestimated. Croker's written legacy of the oral customs of weddings, wakes, factions and festivals gives us a priceless insight into a world long gone.

Crofton Croker differed from his fellow antiquarians in that he took a deep interest in the traditions of ordinary country folk. At that time the belief in superstitions, fairies, goblins and the traditions associated with them were scoffed at and dismissed as pure nonsense by the upper classes. But these oral traditions were an inherent part of Irish country life and were reflected in everyday life and events. These beliefs were handed down orally from generation to generation, and if they had not been recorded by him would have been lost forever in the mists of time.

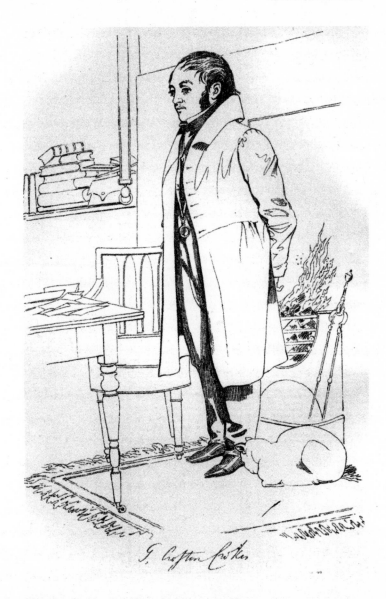

G. Crofton Croker

Croker's surviving letters show that the Grimm brothers, the fathers of the fairy tale, used his work extensively and corresponded with him regularly.

In December 1827, Croker was busy copying some of the old inscriptions from the gravestones at the old cemetery on Ballintemple Hill. One of the old villagers spotted him and became very suspicious of his activities. He was convinced that he had come across a body-snatcher making notes of new burials in the cemetery. The villager ran to Ballintemple and related his story of potential body-snatching. A gang of angry villagers, armed with whatever they could put their hands on, rushed to the cemetery to protect their dead. Luckily Croker heard the shouting and realised that he was the target of their anger. He took flight, pursued by the enraged mob throwing stones, sticks and other missiles in his direction.

Croker also left an important legacy consisting of a manuscript edition of Smith's *Cork,* the first history of the city printed in 1750, which comprised six volumes with notes and annotations. He began the notes on these volumes in July 1830, when he was in England.

He died on 18 August 1854, after an attack of gout, and he was buried in Brompton Cemetery, London. Unfortunately, like so many precious collections, his various books, antiquities and manuscripts were sold by public auction which took two days (18–19 December 1854). It was here that Crofton Croker's extended copy of Smith's *Cork* was purchased by Thomas Hewitt, and eventually it was procured by William Crawford for his library at Lakeland's, Blackrock, Cork.

A Mr MacDonagh, shortly after Crofton Croker's death, said that if he went over the same district in the south of Ireland that he travelled in 1821, Croker would not find one-eighth of the old women able to tell the charming stories about the fairy personage, or rather spirits, which he collected. Unfortunately, Croker's work was not seriously continued until the establishment of the Folklore Commission in the 1930s.

Battle of the Starlings 1621

A mongst the Stowe papers, a collection of manuscripts in the British Museum, there exists a little-known account of a traveller's description of Ireland. In 1620, Luke Gernon, the author of *A Discourse of Ireland*, gives an early description of the city of Cork. His account is not very flattering but it gives us an insight into how a stranger perceived the city at the time. Cork, he stated, was a port by the sea but stood in a bog and was unhealthy. Gernon goes on to describe the stone walls and a quarry of red marble which gave the town a ruddy colour. He noted that the cathedral was in a dilapidated condition, but the town was well populated and compact. He concluded by stating that: 'There is nothing to commend it but the antiquity, and nothinge dothe disgrace it so much as theyr obstinacy in the antick religion.'

The subject of religion came to the fore in the following year with the vicious, unnatural aerial combat of a normally docile species of bird. This strange phenomenon took place over the skies of Cork in October 1621. The remarkable event was recorded in a pamphlet printed in London entitled *The Wonderfvll Battell of Starelings: Fought at the Citie of Corke in Ireland, the 12. and 14. of October last past. 1621. As it hath been credibly enformed by diuers Noblemen, and others of the said Kingdome.* It was believed by many at the time that the account was largely a work of fiction designed to sell pamphlets rather than to give a true description of the event.

> Letters were received by Right Honourable and Worshipfull persons, & others of good reputation now in London, who were eye-witnesses to the strange occurrence. Initially it had been proposed to print this story earlier, but it was considered wise to wait until the truth were fully certified and examined.

The eyewitness account says:

> About the seventh of October 1621 there gathered together by degrees, an unusual multitude of birds called Stares, in some Countries knowne by the name of Starlings. They mustered together at this above-named Citie of Corke some foure or five daies, before they fought their battels, euery day more and more encreasing their armies with greater supplies, some came from the East, others from the West, and so accordingly they placed themselves. Some twenty or thirty in a company, would passe from the one side to the other, as it should seem imployed in embassages.

On Saturday 12 October, the battle began. It continued 'till a little before night, at which time they seemed to vanish'. On Sunday they were seen fighting 'betwixt Grauesend and Wolswigge':

It must have been quite frightening for the citizens to witness such a vicious airborne assault with birds of the same species fighting to the death. The birds had passed over the city in flocks of twenty or thirty hovering in the air making strange noises flying back and forth. The first battle occurred on the 12 October at 9 o'clock in the morning when the battle took place in remote woods. The following day they seemed to vanish as no starlings were to be seen over the city. Passengers sailing from Suffolk between Gravesend and Wolswigge heard the strange noise overhead and witnessed the very same encounter. The starlings were fighting in the most violent manner.

The starlings returned to Cork city on Monday and so the final battle commenced. The loud screeching amazed the whole city and the air was darkened by flocks of starlings. Multitudes of birds fell, some with their wings broken, some with their eyes picked out and others with bills thrust into their opponent's breasts or sides. The violent assault continued, with birds falling from the sky landing on houses and in the river, wounded and dead, a spectacle never before witnessed in any city. Other species were also affected as it was reported that a kite, a raven and a crow were found dead in the streets, torn and mangled.

In *The Wonderfull Battell of Starelings* the fact that starlings violently turn against one another is read as a sign that God was to make sinners atone for their sins. It was also believed that the city of Cork was randomly chosen as an example of the Almighty's frustration with the ways of the world. It was widely accepted by the inhabitants at the time that this event was a prophecy that worse was to befall the city.

Some years later Samuel Pepys composed the following poem:

But such a battle nere was fought,
by silly birds which have not thought:
In doing ill, nor any mind,
to worke contrary to their kind,
but yet as nature gave them life,
to here they strangly fell at strife.

What now for trueth is publisht forth
Esteeme it as a newes of worth:
And by the wonder of their dayes,
Learne to leave off all wicked wayes,
For sure it is that God it sent,
That of our sinnes we should repent.

Lamentable Burning

Following the battle of the starlings the citizens of Cork were breathing a sigh of relief that no further calamities had followed. But little did the inhabitants realise that in a few short months the city was to be decimated by a catastrophe of immense magnitude. This calamity left over half of the city's buildings destroyed and a large proportion of its population homeless and destitute. This strange coincidence had ballad-writers and Jacobean authors reaching for their quills. Once again the London printers decided to make the most of this occasion and set up their wooden press to print *A Relation of the Most Lamentable Burning of the Citie of Corke, in the west of Ireland, in the Province of Monster, by Thunder and Lightning. With other most dolefull and miserable accidents, which fell out the last of May 1622 after the prodigious battell of the birds called Stares, which fought strangely over and neare that Citie.* This pamphlet attempts to tie events together by rearranging the dates of the battle of the birds to the same day as the great fire in May 1622. If successful, the printers stood to receive a handsome commission from this sequel to *The Wonderfvll Battell of Starelings.*

At the time Cork City's formation was typically medieval and the *Pacata Hibernia* map of *c.*1600 shows the main street with about forty laneways spreading from east to west. The city had many houses built of stone with slated roofs, but the vast majority of houses were constructed of mud, timber walls and thatched roofs.

Friday 31 May, 1622, was a very pleasant day with no suggestion of the terrible event that was about to unfold. Between the hours of 11 a.m. and midday, a thick cloud formation began to develop over the city. The dark clouds gathered and hung over the city, pitching the inhabitants into total darkness. Whilst the frightened citizens stood wondering at this extraordinary spectacle, a terrible clap of thunder and bolts of lightning descended from the darkness. At the very place where the starlings had fought, the eastern part of the city, flames took hold of several thatched houses and the inhabitants fled for their lives to the opposite side of the river. They had not got halfway there when they realised that the western part was also on fire. An abundant supply of water was nearby in the River Lee, but no means were available to transport it to quench the fire. Terrified men, women and children were trapped between both fires, which had now become a raging inferno. Any attempt to save goods, wives or children was in vain and many perished trying to rescue their beloved families. Hundreds ran from the city in sheer terror believing that they too would be consumed in the conflagration. Many ran to fields where the fire could not take hold and across Paradise Bridge to an island adjoining the city. This destitute flock of humanity escaped with their lives but their only possessions were the clothes on their backs – they had lost everything.

The less fortunate were still clinging to life, trapped between the two fires; their only hope was to find refuge in the stone churches. The three churches within the city were quickly filled to capacity with men, women and children terrorised with fear. The fires raged on incessantly and the church occupiers were afraid to venture out. Inside their relative safety, the screams and cries of their fellow Corkonians could be heard as the flames consumed hundreds of the trapped inhabitants. Those who had escaped safely from the city witnessed their houses burning, and wives, children, friends, relatives were missing – the nightmare seemed never-ending. So loud were the torturous screams coming from within the city, that the survivors believed that nothing had escaped the devastation.

The population of the city before the great fire has been estimated by various sources at between 3,000 to 4,000 people. An entry for 1622 in the *Council Book* of the corporation of Cork records that 1,500 houses in the city and suburbs of Cork were burned to the ground and that it was a miracle that the whole city was not destroyed.

The cause of the devastation was the close proximity of thatched houses which spread the fire across both sides of the city. The corporation enacted a by-law on 10 October 1622, declaring that all thatched roofs in the city were to be removed by the feast of St John the Baptist in 1623. Any person not conforming to this by-law was to be fined £40 for each house which remained with a thatched roof.

Following the fire, houses and premises were rebuilt in brick and stone with slated roofs enabling the inhabitants to insure their homes and businesses against the risk of fire. The insurance companies trained men in fire-fighting to extinguish fires on insured premises. If further assistance was required in the event of major outbreaks of fire, the necessary volunteers could be recruited and paid for by these companies. By 1707, two special fire engines were provided to the city. The subject of fire-fighting was again discussed in 1714 when the mayor purchased a good large pipe fire engine of the latest design from Holland.

It was to be almost another three hundred years before the heart of Cork City was devastated by fire again – this time the conflagration was started maliciously by British forces stationed in Cork.

A Cork Poisoner

O ne of the most sensational murder trials ever to take place in Cork City occurred on 14 December 1887. Dr Philip Henry Cross of Shandley Hall, Dripsey, was accused of murdering his wife, Laura. The notoriety of the event was further fuelled by the fact that Dr Cross was descended from a reputable Cork family. He was accused of murdering his wife by administering two poisons, arsenic and strychnine. Five thousand applications to attend the trial were received at the Cork Courthouse and many of these requests came from ladies of quality. The majority of Cork citizens believed that he was guilty and that the verdict of the trial would be a foregone conclusion. The Cork newspapers entered the fray and printed several references to the case which insinuated his guilt. Before the Cork trial, Mr Atkinson, QC for the defendant, applied for the case to be heard in Dublin because of the hostility shown to Dr Cross in Cork. This appeal was refused.

On the day of the trial, Dr Cross was brought from Cork Jail looking quite shaken, although he was dressed flamboyantly in a green tweed suit with a yellow scarf. When the clerk of the court read the charge Dr Cross replied in a firm voice 'Not guilty'. The jury was formed, but six of the jury were challenged by Dr Cross' legal team on grounds of religion. The prosecutor, Mr John Gibson, QC, opened the case and he spent much of his time attacking Dr Cross' character, giving much detail of his illicit love affair with his children's governess, Effie Skinner. The evidence which followed gave a jaundiced view of Dr Cross' career and subsequent affair with the young governess.

In 1868 Dr Cross had met an English lady by the name of Laura Marriott and a year later they were married in St James' church, Piccadilly. From the outset her wealthy family did not approve of the marriage to this gruff Irishman. Laura had a dowry of £50,000, which she received in instalments over ten years, and she received a further small income from her brother. Dr Cross had spent some time in the British army, rising to the rank of major, and received a pension of £200 per year. He also inherited the sum of £5,000 from his father-in-law and he had a reasonable income from his tenants and farmland. He could not be described as being extremely wealthy and his marriage had brought with it badly needed wealth. The couple spent many years in Canada and Laura had five children, two boys and three girls.

In 1883, the arrogant Dr Cross was boycotted in Ireland because of his ill treatment of a tenant. Even the local gentry disowned him, resulting in the collapse of his stud business. The local hunt, the 11th Hussars, would not allow him to hunt with them and his labourers refused to work his land. As a result his resources were severely drained and his social standing was in tatters. His wife, Laura, became miserable and depressed, and she left for England on a long holiday to see her family. Upon her return her health had deteriorated further, she became prone to fits of fainting and believed she had a fatal heart condition. Meanwhile Dr Cross became a frequent visitor to one of his few remaining friends Captain Caulfield, JP, who lived at Classis, near Ovens. It transpired that the main attraction was a beautiful twenty-one-year-old governess, Effie Skinner, who worked for the Captain, with whom Cross quickly became enamoured.

Events were set in motion which saw Miss Skinner employed as Dr Cross' children's governess at Shandley Hall. The tension within the house soon became unbearable as Laura realised that her husband was totally infatuated with Effie. After three months of anguish, Effie was forced to leave, but Dr Cross pursued her. In March 1887 he left on the pretext of going to the races at Punchestown but instead he spent two days with Effie Skinner at a Dublin hotel. The doctor became careless and began to write love letters to Effie.

Laura, suspecting her husband's infidelity, quarrelled with him all the time and her health deteriorated further. Within a short time she was experiencing severe stomach cramps even though her husband was treating her for typhoid fever, an illness which showed no such symptoms. On 2 June 1887, Laura died an agonising death and her husband signed the death certificate himself. The funeral was a hasty affair and she was buried at the unceremonious hour of 7 a.m. with very few people attending the funeral.

Just fifteen days later Dr Cross married Effie Skinner (who was three months pregnant) at St James' church, Piccadilly, the very same church where he had married

Laura. Several weeks passed before the newly married couple returned to Shandley Hall. Rumours and suspicion followed them and letters were sent to the police accusing Cross of foul play in relation to Laura's death.

The police were forced to act, so Laura Cross' body was exhumed and unexplained traces of arsenic and strychnine were found in her body. Dr Cross was the only suspect as he had a powerful motive and the expertise to dispose of his wife. He was remanded in the Bridewell, Cork, until he was finally transferred to Cork Jail. The evidence was overwhelming, Dr Cross was extremely disliked, and he had crossed the social barriers of his day by having an illicit love affair with a girl young enough to be his daughter. There could be only one outcome. Judge Murphy sentenced Dr Philip Henry Cross to death by hanging and the execution took place on 10 January 1888.

Effie Skinner, his new wife, slipped quietly away to England where she vanished into obscurity.

St Anne's Shandon

The old parish church of St Mary's which was located at the bottom of Mallow Lane (now Shandon Street) had become too small to accommodate the rising population of worshippers. The earliest reference to the building of a new church, St Anne's, to serve the parishioners of the newly created parish at Shandon, is recorded in the *Council Book* of the corporation of Cork. On 20 February 1722, a plot of ground measuring eighty-six by eighty feet was allocated by Cork Corporation to Rev. Peter Brown, Lord Bishop of Cork and Rosse, for the building of a new church and churchyard in Shandon. A sum of £100 was donated towards the building of the new church by the city fathers. The chosen site was located in a strategic position overlooking the city.

On 18 May 1749, a hundred guineas was contributed by Mr Francis Carleton and Mr Riggs Falkiner towards the casting of the bells which were to be installed in the steeple of St Anne's church. The foundry of Abel Rudhall cast eight bells in 1750. The following inscriptions appear on the bells:

1. God preserve the Church and King.
2. When as you ring we sweetly sing.
3. Health and prosperity to all our benefactors.
4. Peace and good neighbourhood.
5. Prosperity to the City and trade thereof.
6. We were all cast at Gloucester England.
7. Since generosity has opened our mouths, our tongues shall sing about its praise.
8. I to the Church the living call and to the grave do summon all.

On 7 December 1752, the bells first rang over the city on the marriage of Henry Harding to Catherine Dorman. Bell No. 8 (the original tenor bell which dates to 1745) was re-hung in the steeple of St Mary's, Shanakiel.

St Mary's parish appears to have been of significant importance with regard to civic duties; for example the large sum of £40 18s 9d was distributed in 1759 to the poor of the parish from the legacy of Rev. Dean Ward. The church silverware consisted of two silver flagons, two silver chalices and two silver patens, one which was used to collect alms for the poor. Two shillings and two pence was spent on providing a lock and keys for the stocks which were located at St Mary's church. In 1761 the church was undergoing further refurbishments as the organ was in a poor state of repair and the sum of £11 7s 6d was to be raised from the parishioners. The parish fire-fighting equipment and fire engines were housed in a specially constructed building. In 1771, by order of the corporation, a committee was formed to badge the poor, thus allowing them to beg within that parish.

The pepper-box-shaped tower rises far above the city and this striking landmark is still visible from all angles today. The tower is distinguished by the fact that two sides are constructed of red sandstone and two of white limestone. It is believed that the sandstone was recycled from the ruins of Shandon Castle and that the limestone was taken from the ruins of the Franciscan Abbey at the North Mall. A local rhyme went as follows:

> Partly coloured like its people,
> Red and white stands Shandon Steeple.

The impressive weather vane symbolised Cork's once famous fishing industry. The enormous gilded salmon is eleven feet three inches in length and it soars one hundred and seventy feet above ground level. The viewing platform on the tower is one hundred and twenty feet high, enabling visitors to obtain a panoramic view of the city.

In 1843 it was proposed by Cork Corporation to erect a public clock on St Anne's, Shandon, as many working-class people did not have time pieces. The medical profession supported the erection of the clock, as they believed that many poor people were in danger of poisoning themselves by taking their prescribed medicines at the wrong times. James Mangan of Patrick Street won the competition to design and manufacture the clock. To this day the city council is responsible for the maintenance and repair of the clock. It was not installed until 1847 and became known affectionately as the four-faced liar. The hands of the clock appeared to have a mind of their own, especially in high winds, as the hands showed different times on each clock face until reaching the hour where they were in tandem. The mechanism of the clock weighs an astonishing two tons and each dial is fourteen feet in diameter. The inscription on the works of the clock reads:

> Passenger measure your time,
> For time is the measure of your being.

The graveyard houses the vault of the Mahony family where Father Sylvester Mahony lies buried. He composed the famous poem, 'Bells of Shandon', under the pseudonym Father Prout, which immortalised this famous church. In another grave, Rev. Arthur Hyde, the first rector of St Anne's and great-great-grandfather of Dr Douglas Hyde, the first president of the Irish Free State, is buried.

Failing Banks

F alkiner's Lane (now Opera Lane) recalled the old private banking firm which existed in Cork in the late 1700s. Falkiner's Bank was founded between 1760 and 1768 by Riggs Falkiner, the son of Caleb Falkiner, a Cork merchant. Stephen Mills became a partner shortly afterwards and the bank was listed as Falkiner & Mills and was situated near the old custom house (now the Crawford Art Gallery). On 28 July 1768, an advertisement was placed in the *Cork Evening Post*, seeking banknotes which were lost between the city and Killcreaght. One of the banknotes was from the firm of Riggs Falkiner and Stephen Mills, Esqrs, and shows that the bank was clearly in operation by this date. The £50 note had the serial No. 884 and was dated 15 April 1765 and a reward of five guineas was offered for its return.

Following the death of Mills in June 1770, the bank continued to operate and became Falkiner's Bank. By 1776, Falkiner had entered into partnership with Charles Leslie and Richard Kellet, two rich Cork merchants. The bank seems to have prospered as another partner, Dr Bayley Rogers, joined the firm, the name changing again to Falkiner, Rogers, Leslie & Kellet. Dr Bayley Rogers died in 1786 and two more partners joined the firm, which then included Sir Riggs Falkiner, Sir James Cotter, Charles Leslie, Sir Richard Kellet, Knt, and Richard Kellet, Esq. (his son). Charles Leslie remained a partner from 1790 until 1797.

A contemporary *Cork Directory* for 1795 records the hours of business as:

> The hours of attendance from 10 to 2 o'clock and on post days, from 5 o'clock in the evening to do post business only. Their holydays, Jan 1, 6, 18, 30; Ash Wednesday; March 17; Anniversary of Mary; Good Friday, Easter Monday and Tuesday; May 1, 29; Whitsun Monday and Tuesday; June 24; July, 12; August, 12; September 22, 29; October 23, 25; November 4, 5; December 25, 26, 27, 28; and if any holyday falls on a Sunday, it is kept on the Monday following.

The year 1793 appears to have been a period of financial uncertainty due to fears of a French invasion, which caused a run on the Cork banks. It appears that their rival Robert's bank was badly affected, but Falkiner's Bank remained financially viable. The assurance of having someone of Sir Riggs Falkiner's calibre involved, both through his political and mercantile connections, strengthened the bank's position. A similar crisis happened in 1797 which affected private banks as far as England and Scotland, yet again Falkiner's Bank traded as normal.

Following the death of Riggs Falkiner in 1799, the bank's new owners changed the name to Cotter & Kellets. On 29 March 1799, three partners were involved in the firm and upon its re-registration, on 14 July 1800, the list comprised Sir Jas Laurence Cotter, Bart, Sir Richard Kellet, Richard Kellet and William Augustus Kellet. The bank issued notes for various values – guinea and thirty shilling notes were circulated widely. In 1895, Robert Day had in his collection a silver note from Falkiner & Kellets, Cork, 18 December 1799, to the value of 6/–. It has been estimated that £131,630 was the average active circulation over a six-month period. The enormity of this figure versus the level of bank trading suggests that the over-supply of bank notes was responsible for the ultimate demise of the bank. On 8 June 1809, the bank failed to open and all trading was suspended.

According to the *Limerick Chronicle*, 10 June 1809:

At the meeting which was attended by 'Almost all of the respectable population of Cork and a very considerable body of Country gentlemen', and which 'filled the City Court House', it was stated on behalf of the partners that the actual engagements of the Bank with the public amounted to £447,000. To meet this sum the securities of different descriptions of National Notes, Bonds, bills etc., in the possession of the bank amounted to £420,000, so that the deficiency to be made good in order to equalise the debts and credits was but £27,000.

Following this announcement, confidence appears to have waned as the banks notes were traded well below their value. A committee was appointed to supervise the liquidation of the bank. In December 1811, legal proceedings were instituted against the bank and creditors meetings were held at the Exchange, Castle Street on 14 January 1812. A committee was formed to enable funds to be raised to finance litigation against the proprietors and trustees. It was suggested that one penny in the pound should be collected and lodged in Newenham's Bank.

The *Cork Advertiser*, June 1820, published the following letter:

Sir,
In the present state of the City, everyone is talking about Banks,

and I wish to call the attention of the public to a fact concerning Cotter & Kellets bankruptcy. They have already paid a dividend of 6s 8d to the pound; they are about to pay another 5/– and a third of 2/6 is expected – making a total of 14s 2d. The law expenses amount to £60,000 – about 7s 9d in the pound. Had this been paid to the creditors instead of to the lawyers, it would have made 21s 11d, and I have no doubt but if proper measures had been adopted in the beginning, that much calumniated Firm would have been able to have paid 25s for every pound owed.

> Sir, yours
> A Creditor of Cotter & Kellets

Unfortunately, for the creditors, matters did not progress any further, and another committee was formed. A bill was passed by parliament in 1820 to assist in winding up the bank's affairs and a meeting was held at the Crown Tavern on 10 April 1821, where the creditors were informed that no further monies were forthcoming. It was not until 1826 that the final dividend was paid. The creditors received a mere 9/6 or 10/– in the pound because vast amounts were paid to high class lawyers in legal fees.

Lotto Fever Hits Cork

It is believed that in 1566, Queen Elizabeth I created the first British lottery – but it was three years later before it was drawn. That lottery was chartered to raise funds for the 'reparation of the havens and strength of the Realme, and towardes such other publique good workes'. The so-called lottery had each ticket-holder winning a prize equal to the price of the ticket. At the start it was little more than an interest-free loan given to the government over a three-year period. Later lotteries played a significant roll in collecting funds for much needed roads, libraries, churches, colleges, bridges, and other public buildings and improvements. Eventually the government sold the rights to sell lottery tickets to brokers, who in turn hired agents and runners to sell them to the public.

In June 1799, lottery fever was in full swing in Ireland and the *Cork Advertiser and Commercial Register* carried an advertisement proclaiming that William Henry Creagh of the Mercantile Office, No. 2 Grand Parade was selling tickets and shares of the greatest variety. Prizes could be exchanged and the balance paid in cash. The same newspaper carried an advertisement from the printer James Haly, at the Kings Arms near the Exchange, selling tickets and shares for the Irish lottery. This lottery offered twenty-seven prizes which were to be drawn on 23 July. These tickets were being sold at reduced prices on behalf of Browne lottery agents, Dublin, and Haly was his Cork agent. James Haly, in addition to his printing and lottery business, also stocked, books, stationary, prints and patent medicines at his warehouse. The medicines stocked were imported from London and there were a bewildering array available to the Cork public.

By 1803, lottery tickets were selling fast as the citizens of Cork were lured by the huge prizes offered, often as much as a lifetime's savings. So great was the demand for lottery tickets that a lottery office was established in the city. The aptly named Temple of Fortune Cork Lottery Office was located at No. 1 Grand Parade. The Irish lottery worked in conjunction with its British counterpart, amalgamating their prize money and thus ensuring enormous pay-outs. On 4 April 1803, there were four top prizes of £20,000. The number of tickets issued was 44,000 and these could be purchased as shares of tickets also. Most people could not afford the entire cost of a lottery ticket, so the brokers would sell shares in a ticket; this resulted in tickets being issued with a notation such as 'Sixteenth' or 'Third Class' and the prize divided accordingly.

The Cork office was a subsidiary of the main business which was located at Dame Street, Dublin. The proprietors, Messrs Walkers, assured the public that all the prizes and other claims would be paid on demand. Such was the extent of business that government and Bank of Ireland bonds were lodged as security by the Cork office. It appears that, some time earlier, unscrupulous individuals set up a business selling lottery tickets in the city. When the lucky winner went to collect his winnings, he discovered that the seller had vanished with the money. To make the scheme more attractive in 1803, thousands of prizes, ranging from £20 right up to the jackpot, were offered. The Cork office proudly announced that since its commencement, the Irish firm had handled £380,000 in tickets and prizes.

The printing establishments of Cork City worked with the various lottery concerns. In the early 1820s, John Bolster, whose business was at No. 7 Patrick Street, was the state lottery agent. He composed this little ditty to promote his lottery business:

> Here fortune from her golden throne,
> Propitiously on all looks down,
> To public notice she reveals,
> The weighty burden of her wheels,
> Prompt to disperse heretofore,
> The treasures of her glittering store,
> Which in a few revolving rounds,
> Bestows some hundred thousand pounds.

And so it was that John Bolster, with poetic licence, bedazzled the Cork public into parting with its money to spin the wheel of fortune. But this venture was short-lived, as gambling became a liability when the government was unable to control the many private lotteries which appeared each year. Finally in 1826, the British parliament passed an act declaring all lotteries to be illegal. It must have been quite ironic for John Bolster to see his lucrative business dissolved by an act of parliament as he was the crown printer in Cork, responsible for printing and selling copies of these laws.

Scandals, News and Gossip

C ork is credited with being the first city within Britain or Ireland to print a newspaper. The notorious Oliver

Cromwell was accompanied by his printer, who set up his press in Cork for propaganda purposes and *The Corke Mercury* was printed and published in 1649. This first newspaper resembled a broadsheet and, unlike later newspapers, contained military dispatches.

Cork had its own share of newspapers with titles such as *The Cork Chronicle, The Corke Journal* and *The Hibernian Chronicle*. By 1774, Irish and provincial newspapers had become quite expensive as the government had imposed a tax of one halfpenny on them, which rose to two pence by 1798.

Printers in the eighteenth century, in common with other businesses, had signs hanging over their premises advertising their particular wares. These signs hung precariously from shop fronts, glamorising somewhat ordinary businesses. Artistic paintings of famous literary heads were a common sight and Homer, Cicero, Pope, Swift, Shakespeare and other celebrated authors swung lazily in the breeze. William Flyn had the gaudily painted head of William Shakespeare advertising his print works at the Exchange, Castle Street. Flyn was the printer and publisher of a well-known Cork newspaper *The Hibernian Chronicle*, published on Mondays and Thursdays, priced at one penny (this was before the government's punitive tax on newspapers). The first issue was printed on Monday 3 October, 1769.

Newspapers for the most part contained general news, including the latest political and court news. The addition of gossip and scandal from London was sure to increase circulation. Local and notable deaths and marriages were also included, but births were seldom announced. Letters to the printer were also published, as was local poetic verse which was a favourite with the ladies. Advertisements were most welcome as they provided much-needed funds to subsidise the printing costs of the newspaper.

These newspapers give an insight into the social life of the Cork citizens of the time. One advertisement announced that a select performance by the musical society, was to take place at the Assembly Rooms on Wednesday 3 October, 1769. The conductor was a Mr Arne and a young lady was to provide the vocals for this musical extravaganza. Mr Handel's 'Coronation Anthem' was chosen for the grand finale. After the concert, a ball was to be held, and tickets could be obtained from the conductor Mr Arne. The tickets, priced at three British shillings, could also be obtained from Mrs Bunnel's, Coach Street, or alternatively at the Exchange Coffee House, Castle Street. All proceeds were to go to various Cork charities. The music in vogue at the time consisted of Handel's overtures, Corelli's concertos, various sonatas and Vivaldi's select harmony. Patrick Reynold's of Fish Lane advertised the following musical instruments for sale: forte-pianos, guitars, violins and strings for same. The accessories comprised sheet music, good harpsichord wire, oboe reeds and fiddle pins.

Of course the young ladies of the day could not survive on music alone. Cookery lessons were available from Sarah Reeves, a professional pastry cook at Tuckey's Quay. Here the latest methods of pickling, preserving, raising paste, pinching napkins and all manner of household management were taught. Ms Reeves was also prepared to travel to ladies' houses to teach these very necessary culinary skills.

Shop signs had become a nuisance as almost every shop in Cork City had its own sign. Woollen goods could be purchased at the Unicorn and Shuttle between Broad Lane and the Exchange. Other notable signs were the Blue Hand and the Golden Horseshoe, just inside the North Gate Bridge. Linens, hosiery and other goods were to be had at The Golden Ball, Castle Street, and The Unicorn near St Peter's church. The sign of The Raven was located opposite Christchurch whilst the sign of The Three Nuns was at Hammond's Marsh. One of the most frequented ladies up-market establishments was the Three Kings near the Exchange, which stocked rich silks, silk damask and satins of the latest fashion.

Every trade was more than represented: jewellers, book-sellers, hotels, grocers and bakers all displayed their signs. In fact so many premises used this method of advertising that one was confronted by signs hanging from buildings everywhere, at various heights and of irregular size. Something had to be done to eliminate the hazards caused by these wind-powered placards. As the problem of sign pollution grew, an act of parliament was passed prohibiting this method of advertising and mayors and sheriffs had the power to order the removal of all encroachments or nuisances in the streets or lanes of Cork, or to have them removed at the expense of the owners. This spelled the death knell for the colourful and quaint advertising signs of olde Cork.

Debtors Incarcerated

In days gone by Cork had two prisons. One was located at the North Gate Bridge, whilst the other was at the opposite end of the city, at the South Gate Bridge. According to Dr Charles Smith, the North Gate Jail was built about 1715 and was a handsome jail built of hewn stone, well arched and vaulted to prevent fire. This jail was built about the same time as the old stone North Gate Bridge. It is believed from fragments excavated from the former jail, that it was constructed from recycled sandstone.

The South Gate Jail was built about ten years later and it served as the county jail. A four-storey building with a wide arched entrance, in 1752 it was described as a rustic building which appeared more like a palace than a jail.

Of course, no matter how well a prison is constructed or how well guarded it is, the ambition of every prisoner is to try to escape from captivity. In January 1773, prisoners in the city jail attempted to make their escape by cutting a square out of one of the steel windows. Having achieved their aim of making an escape hatch, they foolishly argued as to who should make their escape first. The city jailer heard the arguing and blocked their escape route.

Another escape plan was hatched in November 1774, when a prisoner by the name of Daniel Canty successfully escaped by cutting the iron window bars and lowering a rope onto the street below. The guard ran after him, but in the confusion an innocent man was accosted and deposited in a cell whilst Canty escaped.

A city jailer, Benjamin Bonsworth, was tried and convicted of failing to carry out his lawful duty. The case concerned Timothy Bourke who was to be branded with a hot iron for offences committed. Bonsworth, whether he was bribed or intimidated, did not carry out the sentence and used a cold iron which did not have the desired effect. The jailer found himself on the wrong side of a prison cell and he was fined the substantial sum of £40.

In 1787, John Callaghan and some fellow conspirators attempted to set fire to the prison. They were observed by one of the guards, arrested and incarcerated in the prison that they sought to destroy.

One of the earliest references to the North Gate Jail occurs in October 1621 in the *Council Book* of the corporation of Cork which was edited by Richard Caulfield. An honest person was to be appointed by the sheriff to undertake the supervision of the prisoners of the city. Securities were to be deposited by the jailer as a bond to ensure his trustworthiness. The jail was not yet constructed, but Donogle Merfield was given the position of overseeing the erection of the North Gate Jail. This position was to last during his lifetime and it was officially sanctioned under the common seal of the council. On 31 March, the county jail was enlarged over the east gate towards the west wall of Alderman Wright's and Partners Quay. An arch was created giving free passage to the south river.

Prisoners committed for bad debts were treated

differently from the rest, as they were totally dependent on their friends and the charitable public for food and other necessities. On 13 September 1770 the debtors in the North Gate Jail made an appeal:

> The debtors in North Jail being in a famishing condition most humbly supplicate succour and relief from the charitable and well disposed. Benefactions will be received from the clergy who attend the jail.

Their prayers were obviously answered as shortly afterwards twenty debtors offered their sincere thanks to the mayor of Cork for a carcass of beef and some fish. Dr Blair had donated a heifer and Rev. Sandeford contributed bread to the value of one guinea.

In 1774, Henry Sheares, the well-respected Cork banker and father of John and Henry Sheares, founded a society for the relief and discharge of persons confined in jail for small debts. The following year a second door was inserted in the South Jail to separate debtors from common criminals. Thirty-six persons were assisted by the society from June 1776 over a period of just one year. But by 1782, conditions at the South Jail had deteriorated to the point that the debtors were reduced to drinking the naturally salty water found there to slate their thirst. Consequently, many of them became ill and the manager of the pipe water company was petitioned to provide fresh water.

There was another side to both prisons, where the jailers were earning a nice income on the side by providing extra facilities. Intoxicating liquor was provided to prisoners who could pay for this extravagance. Some prisoners could earn money from the better-off prisoners, who employed them as servants and paid them a little money. Gambling was another nice little money spinner, and the jailers received a commission from wealthy prisoners for turning a blind eye to this illegal activity.

A government report of 1823 described the old City Jail as being a disgraceful ruin and a public nuisance in the city. Amongst the staff was a person who had the dual role of sweeper and executioner, and he received £12 7s for his trouble. One can only imagine the executioner carrying out his duty and then hurrying off the scaffold to carry out his cleaning roster.

By 1832, an act of parliament was passed abolishing imprisonment for debt, much to the relief of Cork debtors.

Rebuilding the Cathedral

R ev. John Gregg, Bishop of Cork, Cloyne and Ross, was instrumental in rebuilding St Finbar's cathedral. At a meeting convened at the Imperial Hotel on 8 March 1864, it was unanimously decided to further the cause of erecting a new cathedral to replace the old one. Bishop Gregg addressed the meeting and with these words he inspired the congregation:

Now my friends would you be satisfied if I put down one hundred pounds. Would that be a good beginning? Take one thousand pounds. Let us go on in the strength of the Lord and we will have our cathedral built.

Tradition has it that St Finbar built his early church on the site of the present cathedral. It is believed the church, like many similar buildings, was a primitive structure. An early cathedral was constructed on the site. The two lower storeys seem to have been part of a twelfth-century church and to this various additions were made over the years. An upper storey was added in 1676 at a cost of £560 and a spire was added just after the siege of Cork in 1691. In 1735, a new cathedral was built in the renaissance style.

Thomas Lane, who was skilled in the art of photography, extensively photographed the old cathedral before its demolition. The learned Dr Richard Caulfield provided the research material and a beautiful book entitled *Vetusta Monumenta Corcaige,* containing nine photographs, was published in Gloucester by the Society of Antiquaries in 1866. The early chapter of the book provides invaluable information concerning the history of the church. An entry for 17 March 1636 records that, 'Martine is to repair and keep staunch the roof of the chancel body.' Burials appear to have been a method of raising much needed maintenance funds, as twenty shillings was paid for each burial in the nave and isles of the cathedral. In April 1677, the mayor of Cork was interred in the south isle, reflecting his prominence and wealth.

Legend has it that Bishop Lyon married the poet Edmund Spenser to his second wife on 11 June 1594 in the original cathedral. The following verses were written by Spenser to celebrate the marriage ceremony:

> Bring her up to the high altar that she may,
> The sacred ceremonies there partake,
> That which do endless matrimony made,
> And let the roaring organs loudly play,
> The praises of the Lord in lively notes,
> The choristers in joyous anthems sing.

During the siege of Cork in September 1690, the cathedral was occupied by English troops under the command of Lieutenant Horatio Townsend. The Irish artillery under General O'Neill fired upon the steeple and a twenty pound shot of cannon struck it, causing serious damage. During the demolition of the old cathedral, the cannon ball was found embedded in the stonework. This relic of the 1690 siege is currently displayed in the south transept of the present-day cathedral.

The building of a new cathedral caused much excitement in the city and in 1862 a prospectus was printed. A competition was announced for the best design and prizes were offered for the first and second winning entries. One stipulation for the design was that the building costs were not to exceed £15,000. On 20 January 1863, the ambitious plans of William Burges were selected. Bishop John Gregg became its patron and a grand total of £6,700 was promised by subscription. The work of the demolition of the old cathedral commenced under Robert Walker of Cork, and later transferred to the firm of Messrs Gilbert Cockburne & Co., Dublin.

When the old cathedral was being demolished in 1865 a beautiful early English doorway was removed and rebuilt into the south wall of the churchyard in Dean Street.

During this time the rebuilding committee was working at full pace raising the necessary funds for its completion. By October 1868, £34,519 had been raised. The initial estimate had proven to be wildly off the mark as Burges ambitious plans spiralled totally out of control. By 1870, the cathedral, which was due to be consecrated, looked unfinished, even unsightly. The lower towers were covered with temporary roofs and very little of the ornate carving seen today, had been completed. On St Andrew's day 1870 (30 November), the great consecration ceremonies took place over a three day period. By September 1873, £40,000 had been spent, leaving only £500 in the bank. The fundraising was in crisis and the grand towers had not even commenced. The project became a bottomless pit as far as money was concerned; few believed that the cathedral would ever be completed.

Just as it appeared that the scheme was hopeless, two of Cork's wealthiest citizens came to the rescue: Francis Wise, the distiller, and W.H. Crawford, of brewing fame, donated £30,000 between them. The project was back on track once more and Mr Delaney was appointed as the contractor for the building of the vast towers. In 1877, Bishop Gregg announced that Mr Crawford had donated a further £8,300 to enable the completion of the carving on the west front. On 6 April, Bishop John Gregg had the satisfaction of laying the topmost stones of the western towers and spires. Less than a month later he was dead; a massive congregation attended his funeral service and the cathedral was filled to capacity. The good Bishop had almost seen his beloved cathedral reach its realisation.

By the time of its completion the project had gone massively over the initial budget of £15,000. In fact, in excess of £100,000 had been spent on creating this architectural jewel in Cork's crown. One can only wonder if this optimistic rebuilding project would have commenced if the financial difficulties that lay ahead had been known in advance.

Riots and Faction-Fighting

Cork City, like all large cities, has a history of riots, gangs and faction-fighting.

The unlawful seizing of English-made goods, food riots, and clashes with the military, were all part and parcel of life in eighteenth-century Cork. There appear to have been a number of breakdowns in law and order throughout the eighteenth century, as armed gangs assembled at will within the city.

An entry in the *Council Book* for January 1726 refers to the mayor offering a reward for any information concerning rioting in the city: a mob had run riot within the city, breaking many windows of city houses and business establishments. In an attempt to learn who the ring-leaders were, a pardon was offered to any person directly or indirectly involved, providing some of the main guilty parties were identified.

Informing on fellow conspirators was an extremely risky business, especially if the informer was unmasked. Matthew Callaghan was convicted of robbing Captain Capel at the Cork City Courthouse. As the judge was donning his black cap and imposing the death sentence, the accused jumped out of the dock, still shackled, and escaped. Unfortunately for him his escape was short-lived, as he was recaptured the same day. The day Callaghan was thrown back in jail, a mob assembled in the city and seized a porter named John Sullivan – Callaghan's betrayer had been discovered and now rough justice was dispensed.

Wounded and badly bruised, Sullivan had one of his ears cut off and attached to the gate of Shandon church as a warning to others. His tortured body was discovered in the street and there was little prospect of his survival. The mayor, hearing of this cruel and barbarous act, immediately offered the large reward of £50 for any information leading to the capture of the perpetrator of the crime. A further reward of £10 was offered for naming any member of the mob. Considering the fate of the informer Sullivan, it is doubtful if anyone was foolhardy enough to take advantage of the generous reward offered.

In October 1765, a mob consisting of several hundred people, including butchers and weavers armed with hatchets, cleavers, long knives and sticks, roamed through the city looking for trouble. The cellars of merchants were broken into and searched for meat and provisions which were to be exported. Little was found but empty baskets, which were set alight on Mall Isle (South Mall). The military attacked the mob and seven of the offenders were thrown in jail but released shortly afterwards due to the unrest within the city.

Faction-fighting appears to have been a popular pastime and spectators were never in short supply. In March 1769, a terrible battle took place between the rabble of Fair Lane (now Wolfe Tone Street) and a Blackpool gang. By December of that year it is recorded that the rioting had become so widespread that it was no longer safe for any person to stand near their door without some form of weapon for defence. In January 1772, the premises of a respectable linen draper near the North Gate was attacked. The candles were put out and, in the darkness, the shop was smashed to pieces and large quantities of goods were stolen. The only apparent reason for the attack was the allegation that the draper sold English and Dublin-produced goods.

Another recorded battle took place between the males and females of Fair Lane when they met their Blackpool opponents at a long field near Fair Hill, and fought each other until nightfall. The females were armed with stones and the males were armed with tomahawks, similar to those of the American Indians and probably imported from America. These deadly weapons were up to four feet long with a hook and spear at each end. The combatants were possibly influenced by the stories written by the likes of James Adair, who had spent thirty-six years of his life living with the Chickasaw tribe of Indians near the Mississippi river. Adair had recorded the origin, language, beliefs and weaponry of the Indian tribe and whilst residing in Cork, told stirring tales of his adventures amongst them.

The feuding Fair Lane mob was preoccupied with other matters when two of their female allies were incarcerated in the City Jail. They had been convicted of the murder of a Fair Lane butcher and were sentenced to be hanged and burned. A rumour circulated within the city that the Fair Lane gang would mount an escape attempt. Extra guards were put on duty at the jail to prevent the impending escape. Unfortunately for the offenders, no such attempt took place, and they were dispatched to eternity for their crime.

The faction-fighting between Fair Lane and Blackpool finally concluded with a full-scale battle taking place at a field named Parkmore, the location of which is not recorded.

Bells and Cannons

Stephen Coppinger was a member of an influential Catholic family in Cork. The custom at the time was to send the children of such wealthy families abroad to be educated. The University of Louvain, founded in 1425, was his place of education. A family story, handed down from generation to generation, stated that one day while abroad,

Coppinger went to a merchant's house or bank to obtain money held for him in trust. As he was busy counting his money, he noticed a young Englishman who appeared to be in some distress as he had no money. Coppinger, being in good humour and feeling charitable, decided to help the stranger. He offered a loan of some money to the young man and an IOU was written and signed for the amount due. After a time the debt was paid and the promissory note discarded. Coppinger also received a ring, either as security or as a token of goodwill. This episode faded from his memory and was soon forgotten.

In 1649 during his Irish campaign, Oliver Cromwell arrived in Cork, where he met with no resistance. Cromwell summoned a meeting of the prominent Catholics of Cork at the King's Old Castle and Stephen Coppinger attended with his co-religionists. Cromwell addressed the meeting wearing a broad-brimmed hat which covered most of his features and Coppinger did not recognise him. However, when Cromwell looked into the assembly, he recognised his former benefactor, or maybe he caught sight of the distinctive ring that he had given Coppinger. He called Coppinger to him and reminded him of the good deed he had performed all those years ago. Cromwell sent him on his way free from any harm with all his lands and titles intact, unlike his fellow Catholics. It is also believed that Oliver Cromwell may have stayed at Stephen Coppinger's house at Ballyvolane and made it his headquarters.

Canon Bolster, an old family friend, related another version of this story, recorded in Wright's *History of Ireland:*

Stephen Coppinger was born in the year 1610. His mother Catherine was a member of a powerful Cork family even before she married John Coppinger. John became a very influential figure within the city and he was Mayor of Cork on three occasions. The story goes that Stephen travelled through Holland during the reign of James I. During his journey he encountered a young Englishman who had been arrested for an unpaid debt. Coppinger came to his aid, paid the debt, the stranger was set free and there the matter rested.

In 1649 at the court of claims in Cork, Coppinger was recognised and sent for by Cromwell. Cromwell stated that he could not decide upon the seizure of his property without seeing him. Coppinger was kept waiting by the austere Lord Protector and when he finally saw him he was asked was his name Coppinger. To which he replied yes. Cromwell then enquired was he at a certain town in Holland during a particular year? Yes came the reply. Did you not pay security for a young man's debts at that time? Yes said Coppinger. Then said Cromwell I was that man and you can leave here with your estates to compensate for your payment.

At the time, Cromwell was running short of artillery and he ordered that the bells from the Catholic chapels should be melted down and the iron converted into cannon. There was much protesting, but Cromwell's humour was quite grim and according to Coppinger he said that 'since gunpowder was invented by a priest, I think it not amiss to promote the bells into cannons'.

Stephen Coppinger led a charmed life and always ended up supporting the winning side. In 1668, he successfully applied to the court of claims during the reign of Charles II and managed to retain his lands throughout those troubled times. He died in 1681 and the following inscription appears on his tombstone, located at the east side of the churchyard of St Anne's, Shandon:

> In this monument erected
> At the charge of Elizabeth Coppinger alias Goold
> Here lyeth the body of her dear husband Stephen Coppinger
> chief of the name
> When deceased the 28th
> Day of July 1681 aged 71 years.

Stephen had four strong sons but they did not inherit the wily ways of their father. During the Williamite wars, all the sons supported King James, for which crime they were outlawed and banished from Ireland, their lands forfeited to the crown. His remaining descendants, the Coppingers of Grangecloyne and Midleton, continued to be buried in the family vault until 1847. The family owned several lands such as Coppinger's Acre, East Coppinger's Acre and Coppinger Park. The family name was commemorated by various laneways named in their honour at North Main Street and Pope's Quay.

The Illumination of Cork

On 22 April 1770, the use of public lamps was discontinued in Cork City and some months later the local newspapers recorded that several persons had drowned in the River Lee. It was officially recorded that if adequate lighting had been maintained these people would not have perished. A Cork newspaper of 26 September 1771, warned

Cork citizens that as the long nights were approaching, great care should be taken crossing the old drawbridge at Tuckey's Quay after dusk. The bridge was in such a bad state of repair that it could not be positioned properly at the other side. Gervais O'Leary was returning from his lodgings opposite Shuttle Row at Hammond's Marsh when he missed his step at the little bridge. In the darkness he fell into the channel and met his watery doom.

Further warnings were issued that the journey from Broad Lane to Fishamble Lane through Cross Street was also extremely dangerous at night. It appears that several citizens had fallen into the murky waters near this point.

The corporation of the city was forced into action. However, the provision of lighting for the city appears to have been a contentious issue. In August 1772, a meeting of the citizens took place at Red House Walk on the Mardyke to consider legal methods to free themselves from the new tax for lamps and watch money.

Mr Kent, an employee of Cork Corporation, was asked by his employers to compile a list of the lamps, lamp irons and posts in his possession. By September of that year the corporation had expended the sum of twenty-two shillings and nine pence halfpenny to Henry Wrixon, Jack Jones and Thomas Fuller for measuring the appropriate places to position new lamps. In October of that year, Mr Kent was employed to erect the lamp irons and posts at the spots which had been marked out. An act of parliament was passed which enabled the corporation to erect approximately eight hundred lamps with single burners throughout the city. One hundred and thirty-nine were allocated to the parish of the Holy Trinity, one hundred and thirty-nine to St Peter's, seventy-eight to St Paul's, two hundred and twenty-three to Shandon parish. A further one hundred and sixty lamps were allocated between St Finbar's and St Nicholas', with a further thirty-eight distributed between the North and South Main Streets.

The lamps were to be lit at sunset and burn until sunrise each day from 8 November until 1 May. Fine rape seed oil or fish oil or a good mixture of both was used to fuel the lamps. The glasses of the lamps were to be kept clean, trimmed and snuffed when necessary, at a cost of £1 1s 5d per lamp. Joseph Harris, merchant, was appointed as the official lamp contractor for the city for a period of three years. The contract was lucrative, so a sum of £2,000 in the form of a bond was paid by the contractor to the mayor as security. But all was not well as Caulfield's *Council Book* records:

> Some evil-minded persons broke every lamp outside the South Gate on the 28th of July 1773.

About fifty lamps were broken in the Blarney Lane area exactly one year later. These breakages were to protest against the tax on lamps. However, perseverance won the day and by 1790 the city was illuminated by light from 1,600 lamps.

As the number of lamps in the city increased so did the salary paid to the lighting contractor, Joseph Harris. Over a period of three years from 1773 to 1775 the sum of £3,182

8s 6d was paid to him. The amount collected as lamp tax by the corporation from the seven parishes and the city centre amounted to £1,851 7s 11d leaving a shortfall of £1,331 0s 7d. The balance was paid from corporation funds. Under the terms of his contract, Harris was not obliged to repair the lamps, but as it was in his own interests to keep them burning brightly, so he used a portion of his own money to fix them.

On 24 February 1816, James O'Brien installed a private gas plant at his premises. His shop at Tuckey Street became the first establishment to be lit by gas in the city. He even provided light outside his premises. *The Cork Morning Post* reported that:

> The brilliancy of the lamps, the neatness and novelty of the arrangement, and the extent to which the light was conveyed through his manufactory and workshops excited general admiration.

This new more effective fuel sounded the death knell for the old traditional oil lamps. But the problem of public lighting soon reared its ugly head again. By night the gas lamps did not cast enough light and with the unfenced quays the chances of drowning increased once again. A contemporary account in the *Cork Merchantile Chronicle* records that to survive a night walk through the city had become a matter of family thanksgiving: 'Every stranger who approaches this third city in his majestie's domain does so at the peril of his life.'

Records of Cork

John Fitzgerald was a teacher of mathematics and he lived in Drawbridge Street, Cork. Initially a Roman Catholic he converted to Protestantism, giving him easier access to teaching posts within the state schools. He was employed as a teacher in the school of St Stephen's Blue Coat Hospital, off Barrack Street. Later he became a private tutor teaching in the homes of wealthy Cork merchants. He was also a clerk to John Marsh Esq., the King's commissary at Cork. He is best remembered for being the author of Cork's first *Remembrancer*. The full, and rather unwieldy, title of this little volume is: *The Cork Remembrancer, being an Historical Register containing a Chronological Account of all the remarkable Battles, Sieges, Conspiracies, Invasions, Rebellions, Executions, Fires, Plagues, Earthquakes, Comets, Storms, Revolutions and other memorable occurrences that have happened Since the Creation to the Present Year, 1783, particularly for England and Ireland and more especially for the City of Cork.*

It is unique in that a large portion of it chronicles crime and punishment in the city. Indeed some of the cases described are so gruesome and macabre that it is remarkable that the book was printed at all. John Fitzgerald was present at the death of every criminal and decided to record every minute detail, and he usually marched from the Jail to the gallows. On one occasion he was confined to bed with a severe illness and was unable to attend a local execution. He petitioned the judges to postpone the execution until he had sufficiently recovered so that he could record the grisly event. It is not known if this particular application was successful but he certainly continued to record later executions.

Fitzgerald also kept a diary for the year 1793 which gives us some insight into his remarkable life. He studied the newspapers of the day and was a constant visitor to the coffee houses located at the old Exchange in Castle Street. He dined in the Oyster Tavern at Austin Lane off North Main Street, and at other eating establishments in Fishamble Lane. His diary is filled with entries concerning the weather and his bouts of drinking. On 26 February 1793, he records that Sergeant Cummins was offering the sum of five guineas for recruits measuring five feet four inches and upwards. The recruitment party consisted of a fiddler and a band of fife and drum, accompanied by a horse and cart which contained a tierce of porter to entice new recruits. Cork City was in mayhem because of the large number of people who turned out to watch this spectacle and vast numbers enlisted, tempted in no small way by the sums offered.

There was a severe shortage of food in the city and a great mob followed the mayor and army to the storehouse in Blackpool. The mayor quietened the rabble by promising to open the meal market on Sunday. Old potatoes were selling at 1s per weight (28 lbs) and new ones at 1s 6d. Cornmeal at the hucksters sold at sixteen pence per weight whilst the mayor's meal sold to the poor people at nine pence halfpenny. Circumstances must have been harsh as Fitzgerald was reduced to eating a quart of green peas for his dinner which cost three pence halfpenny. Mutton was available at three pence halfpenny per pound, and it was the cheapest meat available.

Fitzgerald suffered from a severe back complaint which prevented him from having a good night's sleep. On 1 November he records that he paid Doctor Bagnell one half guinea for medical visits. On 5 November, despite five visits from the doctor, Fitzgerald says that 'I was roaring like a town bull all day until 6 p.m. when Doctor Bagnell gave me some drops, which gave me instant ease. Betty Mackey staid up all night with me I was so bad.' His torment continued and Doctor Bagnell prescribed a little porter each day. Irate words came from the doctor on 22 November, warning him never again to become totally intoxicated. He was not to drink spirits and only to drink porter or ale moderately, which was totally against his habitual need for alcohol.

Fitzgerald's desire to record hideous tales continued. He recorded that Philip Clements killed his wife and afterwards in a fit of remorse and insanity, slit his own throat. More trivial happenings were also chronicled, such as when William White, a tobacco twister, verbally abused his son about his dog which tried to bite him.

He also chronicled his drinking exploits at various watering holes within the city, such as Batt Murphy's, where he could drink porter and punch until after midnight for the princely sum of 1s 1d. Mulligan's and Cotter's were also frequented, where card-playing was a popular pastime and jugs of punch and pots of porter were won or lost on the turn of a card. One evening Cotter's greed got the better of him and he charged the princely sum of thirteen pence for two pots of mulled porter. Fitzgerald promised he would never again pay such an extortionate amount and stormed out the door. The proprietor of Batt Murphy's was glad to see him coming and joined the company for a game of cards which lasted until the midnight hour.

Fitzgerald's Easter Sunday dinner consisted of a nice piece of pickled pork, a bit of corned beef, three pigs tails and to top it off, a fine rasher of bacon. John Fitzgerald's final entry in his diary on 31 December 1793 recorded the worst day of heavy rain for the year. John Fitzgerald, schoolmaster and crime chronicler extraordinaire, departed this life in 1795.

Criminals Whipped

John Fitzgerald published his *Cork Remembrancer* in 1783. In 1824 the folklorist Crofton Croker, having read this work, said that the *Cork Remembrancer* should have been entitled the *Cork Criminal Recorder*. Mr Fitzgerald's book contains the details of almost every execution that took place in the city from the early 1700s to 1783. The enormous subscriber list extends to eleven pages, evidence of the book's popularity at the time. Traditionally crimes and punishments were chronicled by single broadsheets specially commissioned by printers and sold on the day of execution of infamous criminals. Newspapers recorded the times and places of executions, ensuring good circulation figures.

Of all the crimes, treasonable offences were dealt with the most severely. On 18 April 1722, Captain Henry Ward and Captain Thomas Fitzgerald were tried for enlisting men in the service of the James Francis Edward Stuart, 'The Old Pretender' and were convicted. The sheriffs of the city, Maurice Hayes, William Owgan and Augustus Carey, were the prosecutors. The condemned men were brought to the place of execution, Gallows Green, where they were hung, drawn and quartered. The following day William Roe was whipped through the city and put in the stocks for uttering the following seditious words 'May King James III enjoy his own again'.

The application of the law was not infallible and innocent people were convicted and executed. In the same year, 1772, two individuals by the names of Ryland and Keating were tried and convicted of the robbery and murder of Isaac Watkins Esq. of Water Park. They were both hanged for a crime that they did not commit. Some time later a William Lyne was convicted of stealing cows and sentenced to be hanged, and with nothing more to lose he confessed that he was also guilty of the murder of Watkins and that he had the blood of two innocent men on his hands. Lyne's confession also implicated two brothers, James and Michael Byrne, and another unnamed individual, in the robbery and murder of Watkins.

Two years later James and Michael Byrne were arrested on suspicion of committing another murder. They were tried, convicted and sentenced to be hanged. The brothers were brought to their place of execution, Gallows Green, so that the death sentence could be carried out. When he was brought to the scaffold James Byrne became quite violent, grabbed hold of the hangman and tried to throw him from the scaffold. Fitzgerald noted that neither criminal showed any sign of remorse. As a warning to others, their heads were spiked on the South Gate Jail. This practice was continued for many years, but the heads of the offenders were sometimes blown from their positions by heavy winds and rolled down South Main Street, much to the consternation of the local inhabitants. The barbaric practice was discontinued following complaints from the citizens.

Some relatively petty crimes were dealt with most severely, especially crimes committed against the mayor or sheriffs, when again the death penalty was often imposed. Following the burglary and robbery of the dwelling house of Sheriff John Terry, wholesale executions took place. On 5 April 1740, Timothy Hurly, his wife Honora, his son Timothy Jr and his son-in-law Maurice Fihilly, as well as their relations Cornelius Fowloe, Michael Shinnick and Mary Bradeen, were found guilty of this crime and sentenced to death. Mary Bradeen pleaded that she was pregnant, and a jury of matrons were summoned to examine her. No evidence of pregnancy was found, so the full rigours of the law were applied. The harshness of the sentencing suggests that this family were persistent offenders. The aggrieved individual, Sheriff John Terry, had the satisfaction of escorting the guilty parties to their place of execution, knowing they could not re-offend.

Whipping was another method of punishment which was administered publicly. In 1750, William Delaney was publicly whipped through the city for abusing William Holmes Esq., the Mayor of Cork, by calling him a rascal and a son of a whore and shouting that he did not care a fart for him. On 16 November 1765, John Bowler was placed in the stocks for maliciously assaulting a soldier. His sentence was to be three times pilloried and three times to be whipped around the gallows from the piers to the North Gate Jail. A rope was to be tied around his neck, no doubt to remind him how close he came to being hanged.

An unusual occurrence took place following the execution of Patrick Redmond, a tailor, on 10 September 1766, for a robbery at the dwelling house of John Griffin. After nine minutes on the scaffold, the hangman removed Redmond's apparently lifeless body, but a theatre actor named Glover succeeded in reviving him. The story did not end there, as Redmond decided to celebrate his good fortune by getting drunk and visiting the theatre where Glover was performing. The audience, believing Redmond to be a ghostly apparition, fled in terror. Strangely it is recorded that this was the third occasion that a tailor had escaped the gallows since the year 1755.

The harshness of the punishments imposed on the poorer classes reflects the methods which the upper echelons of society used to keep them in submission. Seemingly trivial offences, such as petty theft or utterances of disloyalty, could result in a death sentence and hangings often took place based on the whims of spiteful government officials or city dignitaries.

Beggars

The age-old profession of begging thrived in Cork and many writers recorded their observations on the subject, such as this passage from a pamphlet published in Cork in 1852 entitled *A Run through the south of Ireland* by Valentine Everybody Esq.:

> In the year 1852 two beggars were lounging on the footway near Patrick's Bridge as it was too early to ply their trade. Their conversation was overheard; one by the name of a Mrs Fogarty offers a pinch of snuff to her companion Judy and the topic of conversation turns to marriage. Mrs Fogarty was asked, did not your daughter get married recently and was it a good match? Faith then it was a great match as she married blind Darby Driscoll on the Dyke that can make more money than any three beggars in Cork. Did you give her any fortune came the reply? Ah Judy you are after insulting me; there was no child of mine ever married without it. Didn't I give her the best side of Patrick Street, which if well begged, is worth seven shillings and six pence a week.

Every town and city had its fair share of professional beggars, none more so than the city of Cork. Many beggars gathered outside shops to relieve their victims of any loose change, thereby saving them the trouble of dirtying their fingers with coppers. Every lady passing would be admired – her nose, eyes, hair and dress complimented – to obtain the desired result. All the women engaged in this profession were, somehow, widows with an enormous army of hungry children to feed. The names of all the saints in heaven were invoked so that good fortune would shine down on anyone prepared to part with some small change. It was not unusual to hear them cry out, 'Do lave us the price of a candle, to light the chilther to bed, and the light of heaven to you on the last day.'

Success depended on timing and the approach made to the intended target, just as an actor delivers his lines in a theatre. But frequently a blank denial was given and the beggar woman told to go to the poorhouse. The prompt reply was 'Ah! Then your honour, 'tis myself that has the poorhouse to go to.'

Professional beggars often hired children by the day or week; the more deformed or wretched the child, the more money was given. Valentine Everybody records a scene where two beggars met in the centre of the city, one was holding a poor child in her arms as the other eyed it from head to foot:

> 'Where did you get that child?'
> 'I got it in Mallow Lane.'
> 'How much did you pay?'

'I got the child at a bargain rate of three pence a day.'

'Well,' laughed the other beggar, 'three pence a day you were badly caught,' scornfully pointing to the poor wretched child. 'Sure I could have given you two beautiful cripples for only four pence and you would have made far more money from them.'

Negotiations could go on for some time until a deal was struck between both parties.

Mr and Mrs S.C. Hall recounted some of their experiences of begging in Cork in *Ireland: its Scenery, Character and History*. Upon their arrival in Ireland, they were struck by the numerous beggars that were to be seen in every town. Their wit and humour was proverbial, often making comical remarks at the expense of their own miserable condition. All types of beggars, the aged, crippled, infirm and weather-beaten, gathered together on the arrival of their carriage at every town and village. Upon replying that they had no halfpennies, the answer was ready: 'Ah but we will divide a little sixpence between us.' Every imaginable trick was used to obtain money, distorted limbs exposed and filthy rags displayed like a badge of honour.

But the theatrics really began with the imploring, which was generally highly poetic: 'Darling gentleman the heavens be your bed, and give us something', or another favourite was the blessing of the widow and 'five starving children waiting for yer honour's bounty'. Rejection was dealt with instantaneously – a beggar receiving a refusal from a poor law commissioner replied, 'You would have little business only for the likes of us.' A gentleman observed that one beggar had lost all of her teeth, and she replied, 'It was time for me to lose them as I had nothing for them to do.' If a beggar was treated cruelly, a curse in the form of: 'May the spotted fever split ye in four halves', would be shouted to the high heavens.

In the city, beggars did not usually appear in public until nearly mid-day. A lucrative spot to conduct business was near the Imperial Hotel, where a constant supply of potential victims appeared every day. From the luxury of the hotel their constant wailing could be heard: 'Leave us a halfpenny for God's sake for the lone widow and her five fatherless children.' The Halls gave a graphic description of a beggar woman as seen from their hotel window. The woman was there since morning, wearing a long grey tattered cloak, her dirty cap was torn revealing her tangled hair and her left hand supported her right hand in the most imploring posture. She was still there in the evening rolling from left to right in an attempt to balance herself, a sad picture of confirmed and hardened beggary.

During the famine begging reached epidemic proportions as countless multitudes of starving people roamed the blighted countryside. Whole families took to the road begging, as this was their only hope for survival. The situation became so critical that country beggars were forcibly prevented from entering Cork City.

Commercial Buildings

The first mention of building an Exchange to cater for the needs of the city's merchants was in February 1705. The city council ordered that a scaled model be constructed by an able artist. Before the plans were even drawn or submitted, Alderman Crone was canvassing to provide some of the materials for its construction. In fact Crone was prepared to dispose of ten tons of lead cheaply and it appears he was successful as the elegant dome of the Exchange was clad in lead. (Was it Alderman Crone's surname that gave us the origin of the word cronyism?) Twiss Jones was employed as the architect and no expense was spared in its construction, as it was to be the most elegant building in the city, reflecting the status and wealth of Cork's prominent merchants.

The Exchange was built on the former site of Roche's Castle and because of its proportions it extended onto North Main Street. This created a division in North Main Street, resulting in the creation of South Main Street. No goods were to be sold near the Exchange so that public passage would be kept clear for coaches and carriages. The upper room of the new building was to be used as the council chamber and a stipulation was inserted that it was not to be used for balls, dancing or other such modes of entertainment. By 1710 Richard Deeble, a clockmaker, was appointed to maintain the public clock on the Exchange for which he was paid £6 per year. Edward Roche received rents for the lease of the land where the building was situated, but this caused an ongoing battle with the corporation. As late as 1771, Roche's descendants were still claiming the title to these lands.

Because of the location of the city's main commercial building, the newspaper trade flourished. In 1750, Charles Smith observed: 'Here are only two coffee houses, both near the Exchange: they are much frequented and besides the English papers, have most of the Dublin ones.' It was very fashionable within middle-class circles to visit these coffee houses and books, periodicals and newspapers could be purchased from the nearby printers.

By the early 1800s the building had begun to lose its importance, as it was no longer located at the hub of the city. On 25 July 1808, a Royal Charter was bestowed on the Commercial Buildings Company of Cork. In 1809, a group of merchants held their first meeting at the coffee rooms near the Exchange; their object was to form an association to erect a more suitable commercial building, befitting a city of Cork's stature. Each merchant was to contribute the sum of £100 towards shares in the company, the sum not to exceed £20,000. The most powerful and influential merchants of the city became involved: Sir Richard Kellet, Bart, Sir Patrick O'Connor, Knt, Henry Cooper Penrose, Stephen Roche, William Beamish, William Crawford, Daniel Callaghan and Thomas Harvey all put their weight and money behind this bold scheme. In addition, provision for widening, deepening and improving the harbour and river was made by a further Act of Parliament.

Sir Thomas Deane was the architect employed to design the new building to be situated on the South Mall. A coffee room, dining area and a limited amount of sleeping accommodation was to be provided. The building was completed in 1813 at a staggering cost of £10,000 and included the most fashionable lighting and furnishings.

By 1816 it was decided that the facilities at the Commercial Buildings were inadequate and it was decided that a hotel and tavern should be constructed to cater for overseas visitors and those travelling from other parts of Ireland. Sir Thomas Deane was again awarded the contract and it was completed just three years later. The hotel was leased to a Mr Joyce at a rent of £700 over a seven-year period and was named the Imperial Clarence Hotel.

The old Exchange building at Castle Street had outlived its usefulness but continued to function as an assembly room and people's hall. By 1837, it had become quite neglected and so it was decided to dismantle it. Some of the salvaged stone was used in the construction of St Peter's church in the North Main Street.

The Cork Commercial Building continued to function until it was finally closed in March 1948. The premises was sold to the Imperial Hotel who had ambitious plans to sympathetically incorporate it into the existing hotel structure. The old thirty-foot-high reading room was cut in half, with a completely new floor constructed making it into two rooms. A new row of smaller windows was inserted above the high windows of the vast old reading room. The wide hall was modernised and brightly lit and became the main entrance to the hotel. Thankfully the external character of the old building has changed little since Thomas Deane designed it as one of the first of the great buildings erected on the South Mall.

Cork Workers in Conflict

The earliest trade combinations in existence are recorded in Dublin, *c.*1670, but it was to take some time for these to spread throughout the country. This early form of trade unionism was organised to protect the rates of pay, amount of hours worked and working conditions of its members. The control of apprentices and the embargo on those who had not completed their apprenticeship was paramount to protecting the various trades.

These combinations were declared illegal so they met under the guise of friendly societies. In Cork the leading trades, coopers, tailors and bakers, all met regularly to protect their own interests. As early as 1706 the coopers were petitioning the city corporation, bitterly complaining that Irish papists were setting up as coopers within the city and suburbs. These rogue coopers were employing apprentices, providing much needed employment for their fellow Catholics.

The Protestant coopers were up in arms, claiming that they would become impoverished due to the lack of regulation in the trade. Catholics, under the terms of the Penal Laws, could enter trades but only as quarter brothers. Quarter brothers were so named because they had to pay quarterly dues to practise their trade, but they could not vote or hold any office within their society. The corporation passed a by-law that no quarterer of the 'Society of Coopers' shall employ any journeyman, or keep more than one apprentice unless admitted a freeman of that society. If apprehended, the full weight of the law would be applied.

In 1764, James Chatterton, attorney, was paid for attending the justices of the peace for several prosecutions against journeymen tradesmen who had formed illegal combinations within the city. The sum of two guineas was awarded to the sheriff, Arthur Warner, and the bailiff, James Walsh, for their trouble in apprehending several tradesmen who were guilty of forming combinations.

Following the ending of the Napoleonic war between France and Britain, Cork was plunged into a depression. The British war machine no longer needed the vast reserves of men, labour and provisions which Ireland provided. Unemployment was rife and cheap labour was readily available, which ultimately threatened the trades. If a trade was undermined, threatening letters were sent by the combinations to the culprits. These letters took the form of very direct warnings threatening violence or destruction of property. Death threats were not uncommon: one such letter sent to a master cabinet maker by the name of Cox, warned him to prepare his coffin or quit Cork. In 1842, the bakers ran an unsuccessful strike to abolish night baking, but no violence or threats were used.

By the 1860s, several trades such as the local bakers, carpenters and tailors had Fenian sympathies. The trade combinations were an ideal breeding ground for organised nationalism. At the height of the Fenian rising in March 1867, less than half of the workers at Murphy's brewery turned up for work. The previous night they had left the city to organise the rising in the county.

The coopers had the distinction of being the most militant trade society. Over a time span of more than one hundred years they endured many campaigns to break them. They used every means available to them: threats, beatings and destruction of property were all utilised in their bid to get higher wages and better conditions. The coopers were involved in the supply of barrels to the brewing, butter and provision trade so they were a very important body of men, but they were the worst affected by the fluctuation in markets. The coopers were one of the few trades which had the distinction of being involved in a challenge to a duel, arising from a dispute between a journeyman and a foreman. In 1817, a city cooper had the unenviable distinction of being murdered by a bagpipe-maker during a trade dispute; the reason for this is unknown.

The city's tailors were another formidable bunch of men who were against any form of piece work, including the introduction of sewing machines to their trade. The 1870 strike originated in the firm of Keane and Turnbull, on the Grand Parade, when forty-two tailors went on strike over the use of sewing machines. The coopers, as usual, were the first to offer help and solidarity to their comrades, but the employers used every method at their disposal to break the striking workers. It was a prolonged affair with threats, intimidation and riots being the order of the day. Scab labour was imported from London by the employers to break the strike, but this proved unsuccessful. The stakes were high on both sides, but eventually the tailors were forced to return to work after a bitter strike which lasted ten weeks.

The year 1835 was a particularly bad time for trade disputes – the cabinet makers, coopers, and bakers were all involved in separate disputes which turned nasty. A new sinister weapon was unleashed: vitriol (sulphuric acid) was used for the first time. Vitriol had been used by workers in trade disputes in England and Dublin before this. A Joseph McCarthy was transported to Australia for life for throwing vitriol at a cabinet maker whose chest and neck were badly scarred as a result.

In September 1835, two bakers who were probably strike breakers, Abraham Harty and Stephen Herrick, were attacked and vitriol was thrown in their faces. Eighteen men were arrested, with two turning informer, and two bakers were convicted and sentenced to death. This sentence was later commuted to life imprisonment. Twelve tradesmen, consisting of bakers, cabinet makers, coopers, sawyers and labourers, had vitriol thrown at them over various disputes. The injuries were appalling, resulting in horrific scarring of the neck, chest and face. Features were disfigured, sometimes resulting in the loss of an eye and even cases of total blindness are recorded. This practice was discontinued after a short period, as the death penalty was imposed on anyone convicted of using such an inhumane weapon. Gradually trade unions evolved and dialogue replaced violence – both workers and employers settled their differences around the negotiating table.

Perfectly Preserved

The graveyard in Shandon is quite spacious, although it is situated in a highly populated part of the city. The boundary wall is as ancient as the church itself. When the old North Infirmary hospital was being constructed a considerable unused part of the graveyard was set aside to provide for its site. For a long time there was a natural rivalry between the hospital and the graveyard. Thankfully the hospital had the greater success rate. The headstones and family vaults which are still visible are very interesting as many of Cork's prominent mercantile families are buried there. The majority of the ancient headstones were of the upright type and became very weather beaten. Many years ago it was decided to lay them flat on the ground, but time and nature has taken its toll, and the majority of the inscriptions have become indecipherable. However, the remains of a Mr Daniel Callaghan lie buried beneath the clay and it is recorded that he was saved from drowning by his loyal dog. To commemorate this event he had a stone sculpture of his faithful friend, who can still be seen today, erected over the large gateway of his house at Lota Beg.

Some of the earliest tombstones predate the building of the church in 1722. The earliest legible tombstones date to 1687 and 1696. A low casket-shaped tombstone marks the burial place of Joshua Hargraves, the builder of St Patrick's Bridge in 1864. The Mahony tombstone, dated August 1866, marks the burial place of Father Sylvester Mahony otherwise known as Father Prout, the author of the poem 'The Bells of Shandon'. His grave is just eight yards from the tower with the bells he made famous. The poem or satire that eulogises Shandon's bells, belittles the bells of Moscow, St Peter's in Rome, and those of Notre Dame that are all naught compared to those pealing from Shandon Steeple.

Near the doorway to the tower a memorial slab commemorates the tragic death of Richard Skuse, who it is believed fell from the top of the steeple whilst he was working there. Another tradesman, Roger Wallace, met the same fate and is buried nearby.

Some of the inscriptions are worth noting, such as the engraving on the tombstone of Michael Holland and his wife:

Kind father and mother dear
Two sincere friends lie buried here
Free from malice, free from pride
So they lived, so they died.

St Mary's church was situated near the bottom of Shandon Street and was built in 1693 on the ground donated by Henry Lord Sydney, the Lord Lieutenant of Ireland. It was described as a plain but comfortable church. Visible monuments to the dead are not as intriguing as what lies concealed beneath the family vaults deep in the bowels of the earth. About the year 1780, one of the vaults under the church was opened and it contained the mortal remains of the Rev. McDaniel who had been buried many years before. It was discovered that the body was in a near perfect state of preservation and appeared as if just newly buried. News of this miraculous event spread like wildfire throughout the city.

A large crowd of Cork's citizens gathered outside the gates of St Mary's, hoping to gain entry to see this miracle. The crowds were so big that a company of infantry was positioned in the guard-house opposite the church. A sergeant was put on guard near the body to ensure that the remains would not be disturbed. Any potential law-breakers would face the armed militia. The sergeant's curiosity got the better of him and he went to examine the corpse. Not content with looking at it, he began to prod it with his cane. Unfortunately for him, the nose fell off and he was punished severely for his lack of respect. A new coffin was procured and once again the body was placed in the vault.

In the late 1800s, the historian Richard Caulfield applied to the Church of Ireland authorities to have the vault reopened. Upon opening the vault, it was discovered that no trace of the coffin remained, but the body of the clergyman lay on the floor perfect in every way except that his nose was still missing. It was recorded that the corpse would have passed for an Egyptian mummy.

A renowned Dublin physician was invited to examine the vault, including the method of its construction and its contents. The report said that the vault at St Mary's contained certain antiseptic properties similar to those under St Michan's church in Dublin. St Michan's contains the mummified body of a crusader whose remains were cut in half so that they could fit in a coffin. For a time it was believed that the lime in the mortar preserved the bodies, but this theory was subsequently proven incorrect. The extremely dry atmosphere which existed in St Mary's, Shandon, and St Michan's, Dublin, preserved the bodies and prevented decomposition.

Adjoining the vault to the south-east of the vestry there was an enormous crypt. This was the burial place of more well-known Cork families: the Knapps, Hoares and Gibbings were all buried here. Just inside the iron gate of the crypt, skeletons were clearly visible and this was the final resting place of the Westropps and Dunscomes. To the left a stone was inscribed in memory of the Deeble family. This was the burial place of the earliest official clockmaker in Cork – time had finally caught up with him!

During some nineteenth-century excavations, two leaden coffins were discovered with their sides broken open and the remains appeared disturbed. This intrusion was attributed to the search for a valuable family signet ring, buried with a member of the Pearse family.

First Cork Exhibition

T he idea for establishing an exhibition in Cork was first mooted in November 1851. Daniel Corbett gathered a few friends and held a private meeting in the mayor's office. The plan gathered momentum and a public meeting took place at the City Courthouse two weeks later. The initial plan was to hold a local exhibition, confined to the Munster area only, where local crafts, industry and materials would be exhibited. The Mayor of Cork, James Lambkin, and the chief magistrate threw their full weight behind the venture. As confidence grew, the undertaking began to expand from a Cork City and county display to a full grown national exhibition.

On 12 February 1852, a meeting of the Munster Exhibition committee was held in the Royal Cork Institution, and it was officially announced that the exhibition would extend to the whole of Ireland. It was a very ambitious project at a time when the country was reeling from the disastrous consequences of the famine. The question was raised – who could afford to fund such an expensive scheme? It was realised that agriculture alone could not be depended upon and that the way forward was to promote and encourage manufacturing industries.

The reliance of millions of people on a staple food, such as the common potato, had led to utter ruin for the population. Britain's policy of discouraging Irish manufacturing, whilst supporting her own, was catastrophic for Ireland. As far back as 1698, woollen manufacturing was flourishing in Ireland at the expense of British manufacturers. King William was petitioned by the British woollen interests to do something. He boldly announced, 'I shall do all in my power to discourage woollen manufacture in Ireland' and an import duty of 20 per cent was imposed on all broad cloth exported from Ireland. Successive policies, including the penal taxes imposed on Irish glass manufacturers, closed the three Cork glass houses in the 1800s. Other industries were also badly affected and combined with the ravages of the famine, Ireland was in a woeful state in the mid 1800s. It was believed that the proposed initiative of a massive exhibition would propel Cork, and Irish, manufacturing interests into the limelight.

But where would all the money come from to finance this grandiose scheme? The rewards could be great but if the venture failed who would pick up the bill? Colonel Beamish, of brewing fame, and architect Thomas Deane said they were prepared to share any personal liability. The Lord Mayor of Dublin, Mr Darcy, offered valuable assistance by organising an influential committee to help. Private and public subscriptions were solicited; even the aristocracy became involved with Lords Clarendon and Eglington contributing. The steam and railway companies offered free transport for articles being conveyed to the proposed exhibition. Buckingham Palace was approached and Prince Albert gave the royal seal of approval by donating £100.

The object of the exhibition was to promote Irish manufacturing in every form, from lace-making to brewing and construction; even the arts were advocated. Employment was to be its top priority, poverty was to be diminished, taxes lessened. Above all else it aimed to raise the moral and physical condition of the people by encouraging native industry. Initially the exhibition was to be held in the old Cornmarket building which had been frequently used for concerts and other public events. As the ambitious plans advanced, John Benson was employed to construct a massive new building – one hundred and seventy-seven feet in length and fifty-three feet wide. This great building was to be erected on a site near the Cornmarket.

Disaster almost struck the new building when on 24 April 1852, a roof beam weighing one and a half tons, crashed to the floor. Miraculously, considering that the hall was full of workmen at the time, no one was injured. When it was finished, it was the largest hall in either Britain or Ireland not supported by pillars. The centre of the hall contained a large ornate fountain erected by a Mr Langstaff and as concerts were to be held during the exhibition, the acoustics had to be perfect. The sound check consisted of a single bugler situated at the entrance hall blowing a few notes which could be heard quite clearly at the opposite end. The official opening ceremony of the National Exhibition took place on 11 June 1852. The combined vocal strength of the Cork and Dublin city and county choirs accompanied by a large orchestra performed Handel's 'Hallelujah' to the delight of everyone.

Following the many speeches, a signal was given for the artillery in the camp field to fire repeated salvos into the air to proclaim the event open. The total numbers visiting the exhibition exceeded all expectations: from June until September, 129,031 people attended. The season ticket holders numbered 54,936, whilst 74,095 gained admission at the door. In total £2874 13s 10d was raised in daily admissions for the year. Other revenue was generated by the sale of catalogues which raised £95 5s 6d, refreshments made £55 and lectures £32 7s. Banquets and balls were very well supported and £877 was raised by these events. Every possible craft and material, including the latest advances in science, was exhibited. Exhibitors and spectators travelled from the four corners of Ireland and beyond to this spectacular event. The Cork Exhibition of 1852 inspired further exhibitions there including those of 1883, 1902–03 and the agricultural fair of 1932.

Murder of the Lord Mayor

Tomás MacCurtain, Cork's first republican lord mayor, was deliberately targeted and assassinated by members of the Royal Irish Constabulary on 20 March 1920. It is believed that his murder was an act of revenge for the shooting of Constable Murtagh by republicans at Pope's Quay the previous night. Tomás MacCurtain was an enterprising and successful businessman but his strong republican beliefs ensured that he was ear-marked by the British authorities. In the months before his execution, his home and business had been systematically raided by military and police forces. Rumours began to circulate in some circles that the lord mayor was a marked man. *The American Report on Conditions in Ireland* recorded that on 16 March, four days before his murder, Denis Morgan, a republican activist in Wormwood Scrubs prison, heard that MacCurtain 'had been sentenced to death by the Royal Irish Constabulary'.

Initially Tomás MacCurtain was employed as a clerk at the City of Cork Steam Packet Company. He became one of the main driving forces of the Gaelic League in Cork, spending every spare moment promoting Irish language, history and tradition. He taught Irish at the Gaelic League branch in Blackpool. Before the 1916 Rising he had established a successful meal and flour business. He purchased large quantities of meal and flour and resold them to cattle dealers. After the unsuccessful Rising of Easter week, the British authorities, knowing that he was a republican activist, attempted to ruin his business. The British military would arrive at his premises, under the pretext of searching for guns and ammunition. The meal sacks were bayoneted and the meal was contaminated, spilling all over the dirty street.

As a known republican, Tomás MacCurtain was arrested after the 1916 Rising but no charges were brought against him because there had been no uprising in Cork City. He was deported to Reading Jail, and from there transferred to

Frongoch in Wales. This internment camp had been used to detain German prisoners of war during the First World War of 1914–1918. Conditions were terrible and it was not a fit place to confine prisoners of any description.

Night-time raids on his home continued even though he was in prison, often at three o'clock in the morning when his children were asleep. Armed police or soldiers would break into his home armed with rifles and fixed bayonets and turn everything in the house upside down.

On 30 January 1920, Tomás MacCurtain was elected mayor of Cork. According to *The American Report on Conditions in Ireland*, on the night of MacCurtain's murder, the house was surrounded by armed men who shouted: 'Open up quickly or we will break the door in.' Before anyone could react, the door was broken in. Eight or nine men with blackened faces rushed towards the stairs and pushed Mrs MacCurtain violently aside. Two of the group reached the landing and shouted 'Come out Curtain!' When he came out, three shots were fired and he fell to the ground with blood oozing from the region of his heart. Mrs MacCurtain was hysterical and the children were crying inconsolably. A priest and Doctor O'Connor were sent for and within fifteen minutes this brave man was dead. About an hour later the house was raided again, every part of the house was searched by the military who said that they were looking for the perpetrators of the crime – an amateurish attempt at a cover-up.

The historic inquest conducted by Coroner James J. McCabe returned a courageous verdict: that the late lord mayor was wilfully murdered under circumstances of the most callous brutality by the Royal Irish Constabulary under the direction of the British government. A verdict of wilful murder was pronounced against David Lloyd George, Prime Minister of England, Lord French, Lord Lieutenant of Ireland, Ian McPherson, late Chief Secretary of Ireland, Acting Inspector General Smyth of the RIC, Divisional Inspector Clayton of the RIC, District Inspector Swanzy and other unknown members of the RIC. The coroner extended sincerest sympathy to Mrs MacCurtain and her family. The evidence had shown that the murder was premeditated, with a large number of RIC involved. The planning required clothing for the purpose of disguise, faces were blackened and military precision used – all at a time when the British authorities had control of the city under martial law.

The cover-up began immediately when awkward questions were asked in the British House of Parliament: According to *The American Report on Conditions in Ireland*, Sir Hamar Greenwood was prompted by a whisper from either Winston Churchill or Lloyd George to 'say the Sinn Féiners did it'. This defence clearly demonstrates the lengths the British government were prepared to go to, to mislead public opinion. The authorities were challenged to produce evidence of the participation of Sinn Féin extremists, but no such evidence was ever found.

Tomás MacCurtain was lord mayor for just three short months before his death. He had been elected by one of the largest ever majorities and was held in much affection in the city. Alderman Beamish, a unionist, broke down and cried when the corporation passed its resolutions of sympathy.

The funeral was one of the largest ever witnessed in Cork City. Every class and creed attended the funeral. Bishop Dowse the Protestant bishop, the Jewish rabbi, Methodists, Baptists and people of differing religious persuasions, were among the 10,000 people who marched from the North Cathedral to St Finbar's Cemetery where Terence MacSwiney gave a brief oration.

Hunger Strike

Terence MacSwiney was born in Cork City on 28 March 1879. The MacSwiney family were well respected in Cork and his father was a tobacco manufacturer. He attended the Christian Brothers at the North Monastery School where he excelled in Irish and Irish history. Because of the failure of his father's tobacco business, the young Terence went to work at Dwyer & Company in Washington Street at the tender age of fifteen. He was employed for seventeen years with this firm and rose to the position of accountant in 1911. He left Dwyer's and became a commercial teacher for the Municipal School of Commerce. It is reputed that it took several clerks at Dwyer's to do his job.

He soon became involved in writing articles for various

national newspapers. He reduced the number of hours he slept to write and study. His first book, *Music of Freedom,* was published in 1905, a lengthy poem promoting his desire for Ireland's freedom. In December 1913, together with Tomás MacCurtain, Seán O'Hegarty and J.J. Walsh, he formed the Cork Volunteers. Slowly but surely the movement grew until eventually the Cork Volunteers were openly carrying out drills in the Cork Cornmarket yard. His great friend Tomás MacCurtain was a brilliant military organiser, but MacSwiney's talent lay in public speaking and writing. He published his own newspaper *Fianna Fáil,* which he used as a platform to promote Irish nationalism. Needless to say the British authorities suppressed this republican organ after eleven issues.

The Cork Volunteers expected to play a pivotal role during the Easter Rising of 1916, and were armed and ready for action. Then the national head of the Volunteers, Eoin MacNeill, sent messages cancelling the mobilisation of all forces and placed notices in the daily newspapers. This countermand to all Volunteers cancelled all actions for Sunday, but only succeeded in putting the Rising off for a day, and greatly reducing the number of Volunteers who turned out. MacSwiney and MacCurtain were bitterly disappointed, all their hopes and plans were dashed. The Volunteer Hall in Cork was primed for action. Men from different companies had come from country areas and were staying overnight in the hall, but events in Dublin had overtaken the rest of the country. Due to the interception of the arms on board the German boat the *Aud,* and the subsequent scuttling of the vessel, the provincial Volunteer units were very poorly armed.

Threats were made by the British military in Cork: unless the Volunteers in the hall disarmed and surrendered the city would be shelled. To prevent any bloodshed, Dr Cohalan, the Bishop of Cork, offered to broker a deal. The Volunteers, considering their weak position, were forced to hand over their arms to the lord mayor – these were to be returned to them at a later stage under the terms of the agreement. The British military arrested some of the Cork Volunteers including Tomás MacCurtain.

The leaders of the Volunteers were now marked men, Tomás MacCurtain was killed by the Royal Irish Constabulary at his home in front of his wife and children. Terence MacSwiney did not shirk from his responsibilities and he was elected unanimously to replace MacCurtain as lord mayor of Cork.

Being a republican lord mayor of Cork meant that he had to take precautions, as the British authorities were determined to be rid of this thorn in their side. Concealed doors were installed in the City Hall so that he could make good his escape if necessary. On 12 August 1920, the City Hall was raided by a considerable British army contingent of six armoured cars and six lorries full of soldiers. The lord mayor was arrested and charged with having a cipher key to decode military dispatches. He was ordered to hand over his chain of office which he refused; it was then forcibly removed but was returned the following day. When asked if he wished to be legally represented he replied:

> The position is that I am Lord Mayor of Cork and Chief
> Magistrate of this city. I declare that this court is illegal and
> those that take part in it are liable to arrest under the laws of
> the Republic.

He was sentenced to two years' imprisonment, but he declared that he was on hunger strike: 'I will be free within a month either alive or dead.'

MacSwiney was taken on board a British naval vessel in the early hours of the morning and incarcerated in Brixton prison. The prison doctor said that he was in such a poor state he would not survive force feeding. The British authorities tried to keep him alive, their purpose was to defeat him not to make him a martyr. As his hunger strike went on this brave man became headline news. Journalists from all corners of the globe descended on Brixton prison much to the embarrassment of the British authorities. A solitary Irishman was taking on the might of the British Empire by offering himself as a sacrifice for a cause he was prepared to die for.

It seemed as if the whole world was behind him – prayers, protests and appeals, even work stoppages, occurred at home and abroad. As each day passed, the lord mayor became weaker and weaker until, on the seventy-third day of his hunger strike, Terence MacSwiney died.

The British authorities prevented the body going to Dublin, mindful of the events following the Easter Rising. The body was sent to Cork on board the *Rathmore* and eventually handed over for burial. Tens of thousands of people lined the street of Cork as a mark of respect for this great man. The might of the British Empire had been shaken and the ultimate sacrifice made:

Victory is won not by those who can inflict the most
But by those that can endure the most.

Terence MacSwiney

Slaves Jump Ship in Cork

T he *Cork Evening Post* was printed in Castle Street by Phineas and George Bagnell and it consisted of two folio sheets which contained news from Cork, Dublin, Britain and other foreign places. The following extract, 6 April 1769, concerns a reward being offered for the return of a runaway slave:

> A reward of twenty guineas is offered this day for a young negro man, who ran away from his master, Robert Burke Esq. His description is thus given: Name Jerry; 5 feet 8 inches, large boned, well set, but not fat; has large strong negro features, scar on right hand; slightly marked with small pox; had on a light-coloured grey coat, dirty leather breeches, white stockings, and wore a curl behind that matched the other part of his own woolly hair; reads and writes badly, plays pretty well on the violin, and can shave and dress a wig.

Burke, the master of this slave, gave an undertaking that he would forgive him if he returned. Burke was determined the slave would be returned to him. If the poor unfortunate did not give himself up then two leading merchants,

Messrs Devonshire and Strettell, were prepared to make themselves available to track him down for a reward. The outcome is not known, but the chances that this poor man escaped the clutches of his pursuers was practically nil.

By the eighteenth century, African, Indian and East Asian slaves were brought to London and Edinburgh as personal servants. They were not bought or sold, and their legal status was unclear until 1772, when the case of a runaway slave, James Somersett, forced a legal decision. James had escaped from his American owner, Charles Stuart, in England and been helped by those opposed to slavery. Stuart recaptured him and put him on a boat to Jamaica to work on the sugar plantations. However, Somersett's English friends challenged this in court, as there was no legislation for slavery in England. Chief Justice Lord Mansfield decided to release the slave.

It was generally accepted by the legal profession that the practice of slavery did not exist under English law. Unfortunately slavery was a way of life in other countries, especially America, where they were exploited mercilessly, and Britain played a major role in the exportation of slaves. In 1783, the Quakers founded the first anti-slavery movement in America and this quickly spread to Britain and Ireland. Cork Quakers took an interest in the movement because of their strong trading ties with their fellow American co-religionists. By 1787, an anti-slavery society had been founded in London and its aim was to put pressure on the British government to abolish the slave trade in Britain entirely.

Pamphlets began to be circulated in Cork to raise support for this cause and in 1792 Anthony Edwards at No. 3 Castle Street printed a sixty page *Essay on the Slave Trade* aimed at enlightening the Cork public. The West India slave trade was singled out for particular mention and it was advocated that all produce from this part of the globe should be boycotted. Literature and a public ban on produce originating from slave labour were the main weapons in the Cork anti-slavery arsenal. The Cork Quaker and philanthropist Joshua Beale, formed the Cork Anti-Slavery Society in 1826 at the Assembly Rooms in George's Street (now Oliver Plunkett Street). A petition to abolish Negro slavery throughout the British dominions could be signed at Mrs Osborne's shop at No. 6 Castle Street. This also happened to be the location of Edwards & Savage printing establishment, where anti-slavery tracts were published.

In 1830, the members of the Cork-anti slavery society became involved in a case where slaves were being held prisoner on board a ship in Cork harbour. The society was successful in having them released from their bondage. By May 1838, slavery in the British colonies had been abolished by an Act of the British Parliament. The Cork society then turned its attention to the American anti-slavery campaign.

By 1841, the ladies of Cork decided to form their own society hoping that their genteel approach would win the day. In 1846, *The County and City of Cork Post-Office Almanac* records Mr F.B. Beamish and Mrs Beamish as presidents of the male and female anti-slavery societies respectively. Together with the backing of their respective movements, this husband and wife team were instrumental in inviting Frederick Douglass, an escaped slave, to come to Cork to give a talk on the evils of slavery. The Courthouse was filled to capacity, with supporters and the inquisitive jostling for the best seats. The mayor, accompanied by John Francis Maguire, presented Douglass with an illuminated address in his honour. Further meetings were held in the various chapels and his biography *A Narrative of the Life of Frederick Douglass* was selling like hot cakes. Father Mathew, the famous temperance campaigner, also took a keen interest in the abolition of slavery and he met Douglass at some of the Cork meetings.

Unfortunately the famine, which was to decimate the Irish population, interrupted the good work of the Cork anti-slavery societies. The Society of Friends, the Quakers, numbering little more than 3,000, turned their attention to helping and feeding Ireland's starving poor. Despite their limited numbers and resources, their Herculean efforts during that great catastrophe saved thousands of lives. Some 37,000 letters and reports resulted in £200,000 worth of donations being handled by the Quaker Central Relief Committee. At this time the Cork anti-slavery movement turned its resources towards setting up soup kitchens in Barrack Street and Henry Street to feed the starving inhabitants of Cork City.

Revolutionary Doctor

King George III suffered from a mysterious illness in the eighteenth century which was eventually diagnosed as a form of mental illness. There was much rancour and jealousy between the various physicians in their attempts to find a cure, and the fame and fortune that it would bring. One of these so-called doctors boasted that during treatment he knocked the King as flat as a flounder. This assault on the royal personage prompted an inquiry which was held by the House of Lords and led to the improvement of the methods used to treat the mentally ill in both Britain and Ireland.

On 19 October 1745, Jonathan Swift died aged seventy-eight. He had managed to retain some of his sense of humour in his later years, and his last will and testament provided funds to establish in Dublin a hospital for 'ideots & lunaticks' because 'No Nation wanted [needed] it so much.' However the hospital was intended to be more than just a parody, as Swift was also genuinely committed to the care of people with mental illness. His legacy of £11,000 established the oldest psychiatric hospital in Ireland: St Patrick's Hospital in Dublin. Famously, he described his gesture in a satiric poem 'On the Death of Dr Swift':

> He gave the little wealth he had
> To build a house for fools and mad,

And showed by one satiric touch
No nation needed it so much.

The Poor Law Act of 1735 provided accommodation in workhouses, or as they were termed Houses of Industry, for the mentally ill in Cork. A House of Industry was established in 1766 and was situated on the site of the South Infirmary Hospital. On 19 September 1791, the governors of the House of Industry thanked Mayor Richard Harris, Esq., for his wonderful donation of twenty-six flat fish, seven hake, one salmon, twelve lobsters and three baskets of sprats. A leg of mutton had been was seized from a butcher in the New Shambles area and this was also contributed. One can only wonder how much of this fine food reached the mouths of the residents. The mayor was also involved in a fundraising event, to be held at the New Theatre Royal at Princes Street. Money was badly needed for the 'erection of additional cells because of the extraordinary number of lunatics now in it'.

In the early 1800s, the chief officer of the Mendicity Asylum was Rev. John Egan, the superintendent was R. Thorpe and Father Mathew was one of its governors. William Martin, the Cork Quaker who was known as the grandfather of the Temperance Association, was also a governor. In December 1830, there were two hundred and ninety-eight persons in the asylum section, these consisted of one hundred and eighty-one old and helpless, thirty-five working class, seventy-six children and six paupers. On Christmas day three hundred pounds of bread was divided between the poor inmates, a paltry treat to commemorate the birth of Jesus. Two pence was the cost per day of keeping and feeding each inmate. The physician and apothecary, Dr William Sanders, was paid £113 15s per year.

Occasionally tea was purchased, as in the year 1810 when a couple of pounds were purchased for the exorbitant sum of 8s 8d per lb. Bread was supplied only to the hospital and it was only given to inmates on special celebratory occasions. In December 1809, two hundred loaves of bread costing 3d each were supplied to the healthy inmates. Two barrels of ale costing £2 16s 4d were donated to drink to the King's health. Oatmeal was the main diet, as it was cheap and convenient to cook, averaging sixteen shillings per hundred weight. The House of Industry and Asylum was covered by insurance. The Atlas Insurance Company charged premiums at £2 2s 1d for each patient, but due to the volatile nature of the patients within the asylum it was also insured for an additional £1,000.

In 1830, the asylum was described as one of the best models of its kind and this was due in no small measure to Dr Sanders, who ranked as one of the great pioneers of mental illness in his day. His studies enabled him to publish a book entitled *Practical Observations on the Causes and Cures of Insanity,* printed by Edwards and Savage in Castle Street in 1818. The doctor had a special circulating swing made, which could revolve at amazing speeds with the patient inside, either sitting or lying down. These experiments relaxed the patients, thereby helping their mental health.

By 1845 an act of parliament was passed to provide for the building of a new asylum. In 1852, the Cork District Lunatic Asylum, otherwise known as the Eglington Asylum, on the Lee Road was formally opened. The building was designed by the architect William Atkins and built in the gothic style. Due to budgetary constraints a poor quality, dark stone was used which has not weathered well.

The building, facing southwards, resembles a hospital, unlike earlier asylums which appeared like jails. The surrounding grounds comprising fifty-seven acres were purchased for £10,000. The total cost of the buildings, which included a chapel, stables, farm buildings and a gate lodge, was £85,000. Originally designed as a separate building, it became three buildings linked by corridors and had probably the longest frontage of any building in Cork City or county. In 1859, Bryan Cody, in his book *The River Lee, Cork and the Corkonians,* records that the asylum can hold five hundred inmates, the largest of its kind in the whole of Ireland. He also remarks that this should not infer that the people of Cork are more disposed to insanity than those of any other town or city in Ireland of Britain. But what can be said of the good people of Cork who, whilst honouring the Lord Lieutenant of Ireland, Lord Eglington, erected a Lunatic Asylum in his name?

Smith's *History of Cork*

In 1744 Charles Smith, a Dungarvan apothecary, together with Walter Harris published a history of County Down. It was the first extended Irish county history ever published and it was proposed that a series of similar histories would be published. A society, the Physico-Historical Society, was to be established to gather material for the series. Smith spent much time researching the first history which covered his native Waterford. These histories contain detailed descriptions of the land, its natural products, people, natural history, etc. A special series of maps was commissioned, but Smith asserted that he had made his own drawings of maps and claimed them as his own. The maps are very important, as they were the first new updated maps of the counties since the seventeenth century.

A meeting of the Physico-Historical Society was held and the Rev. and Right Hon. Lord Viscount Strongford stated that:

> Mr Charles Smith having laid before the society a manuscript copy of the *Antient and Present state of the County and City of Cork*, with an accurate two sheet map of that county &c. It is considered that the said work be published with the approbation of this society.

The objective of this series was to collect materials on every Irish county, which would then be collected into one complete set, similar to Camden's *Britannia*, to be published under the title *Hibernia* or *Ireland Ancient and Modern*. The book appears to have been hugely popular, as the subscribers list ran to eight pages, totalling over five hundred people. The history was dedicated to the Earl of Orrery, the Duke of Cumberland, the Earl of Harrington, the Lord Lieutenant and the general governor of Ireland.

The inclusion of so many aristocratic names ensured that the book would sell well. Mr T. Croneen, a Cork bookseller, ordered seven sets whilst four of his Dublin counterparts ordered fifty sets between them. This first history of Cork was printed in Dublin in 1750 and it included a large plan of the city. The beautiful panoramic view of the city provides invaluable information on how the city appeared at the time. All the main buildings are named including churches, castles, hospitals and the main commercial buildings. It is quite possible that this view inspired Jonathan Butts to paint his 'View of Cork', *c.*1760. The similarities between Smith's prospect and Butts' painting are quite striking. Other folding views in this history include Kinsale and Youghal.

Twenty-four years later William Wilson, another Dublin printer, decided to publish a second edition, due to the success of this popular work. An advertisement bound in with the second edition states that Wilson was inspired by the same ideals that had inspired Smith to prepare a second edition for Waterford. In 1774 the price of the Waterford and Kerry reprints was six shillings and six pence, the two-volume Cork history was thirteen shillings. The third edition, again in two volumes, was printed by

John Connor, a Cork printer whose business was in Patrick Street. Connor records:

> The constant application for Smith's *History of the County and City of Cork*, and the universal regret that it was not to be obtained, induced the present editor to publish a new edition.

This 1815 edition had two hundred and fifty subscribers, with six sets purchased by a Dublin bookseller and twenty copies purchased by a Bristol bookseller.

These three editions, from the first in 1750 through 1774 and 1815, were republished with very little change apart from new subscriber lists. The subscription lists incorporated in all of these editions give us an interesting insight into the names of the influential inhabitants of the city and county of Cork at the time. The so-called additions were of a cosmetic nature and no real attempt to correct or update the previous editions was seriously attempted. Incredibly, the third edition still featured the original 1750 map of the city. John Connor declared it unnecessary to correct or expand this work, although he did concede that any additions should appear as a separate volume. It would appear that his motivation for not updating this early history was to make money, as revising it would be a costly business. Connor reprinted the Cork, Kinsale and Youghal views from his own plates, but they were not as detailed as in the Dublin editions, as he did not have the original plates and was forced to create his own.

Cork had experienced enormous change geographically between these years, marshes had been built over, bridges constructed and commercial buildings erected. Several maps were published in the following years, notably Rocque's updated map of 1773, Murphy's map of 1789 and Beaufort's map of 1801. These maps show the advancement of the city into the newer areas, i.e. Grand Parade, and Patrick Street which were formerly channels of the river. Unfortunately none of these maps were included in Connor's edition. William O'Sullivan in his *Economic History of Cork* said, 'Smith's work however, is valuable, not so much as a historical work, but as a source of intimate information regarding the state of affairs in or about the time when he wrote.'

Unfortunately, none of Smith's sources are referenced, but the books give us a unique contemporary insight into the affairs of the city and county. History, trade, political loyalties and military campaigns are all covered in Smith's pioneering *History of Cork City and County*.

Beamish *v.* Murphy's

An early deed of 1667 refers to a George Syms who had lately purchased a dwelling house, malt house and a brew house in the city of Cork. These properties had formerly belonged to James Lavallin and changed hands for the princely sum of £70. The brew house was located in the parish of the Holy Trinity, near the South Gate Bridge.

This is probably one of the earliest references to the site of the Beamish & Crawford Brewery. It is believed that the history of brewing on this site could date back to the year 1500. The title deeds of Beamish & Crawford date to 1792, but they refer to Allen's Brewery which existed on the South Main Street site in 1715. The Allens were a very influential family in Cork, as John Allen became mayor of the city as early as 1713. They also had the distinction of having a laneway named after them, which was eventually incorporated within the Beamish & Crawford site.

William Beamish and William Crawford were Cork merchants and they made their money by importing beer into Cork from the London breweries. Tradition has it that having placed a large order with a London brewery, bad weather interrupted their supply. This left the thirsty natives of Cork without their favourite tipple, so Beamish and Crawford decided to purchase their own brewery and have a supply right on their doorstep. In 1791, the last of the Allen dynasty, Edward, died and his property was put up for sale. Allen had been the owner of the city's largest brewery producing some 13,000 gallons per year. Beamish and Crawford purchased this ready-made brewery and began trading as the Cork Porter Brewery.

As time went by the brewery was enlarged and modernised and, in the early 1830s, it had the distinction of being the largest brewery in Ireland. The two partners concentrated on the provincial markets, unlike Guinness who had a huge export market. But Father Mathew's Temperance campaign of the 1840s had a devastating effect on the market for alcohol. The number of small local breweries in the city had been decimated, reduced from eighteen to six. In its heyday the Cork Porter Brewery accounted for the payment of 12½ per cent of the city's rates, an enormous sum. By the late 1850s, the brewery had bought out some of the remaining smaller concerns. This strategy combined with the purchase of tied houses, public houses that were owned by the breweries, strengthened its position. By 1860, the Beamish & Crawford site covered an area in excess of five acres.

Fortunately for Beamish & Crawford, the Guinness brewery had concentrated on the export trade leaving them to their own devices. In Cork, the tied house system was working well for them, ensuring that their public houses sold only their products. This meant that a monopoly existed in Cork and prevented competition from non-Cork based breweries.

But trouble was on the horizon: in 1856 the Murphy family began production at Lady's Well Brewery on Leitrim Street. The Murphys were no strangers to the alcohol business as they had been operating a very successful distillery in Midleton since 1825. Brothers William, Jerome, Richard and James J. Murphy entered into partnership to form a rival brewing concern in the city. Following an unsuccessful venture into ale production the Murphys decided to concentrate on the growing porter market.

Their main opposition, Beamish & Crawford, were unhappy with this new competition which would break their monopoly on the porter trade. The Murphy brothers spent enormous sums of money on their new brewery, ensuring that it was built and designed to the most modern London standards. After just three years in business, it had made significant inroads into the Beamish & Crawford customer base. By the 1880s it had overtaken its rivals, capturing nearly half of the market compared to Beamish's one-quarter. In 1885, James J. Murphy had earned so much money from his brewing activities that he was able to save the Munster Bank from financial ruin. He spearheaded the campaign to establish a new bank in the city and as a result the Munster & Leinster Bank was established. He had saved the city and thousands of depositors and creditors from financial ruin and prevented a run on the other banks.

The Murphys were quite adept at advertising and commissioned Eugene Sandow, the 1891 World Weight-Lifting Champion, to endorse their product. Sandow lifting a horse became their trade mark, associating Murphy's stout with strength. This was forty years before Guinness mimicked this novel concept of advertising. But alas for the smaller breweries these two behemoths of the brewing industry had their sights set on capturing a larger share of the home market. Arnott's brewery was purchased by Murphy's in 1901 and it was closed shortly afterwards, increasing the Murphy's Brewery tied house share by about one hundred and fifty public houses. Beamish & Crawford were not slow to react and purchased their close competitor Lane's Brewery (est. 1758) on the South Main Street acquiring their tied houses. At this time these two breweries had a monopoly on the city trade, accounting for about one half each.

In 1980 Colonel Murphy died and he was the last male heir to the Murphy's brewing dynasty. By 1982, Murphy's Brewery was in receivership, facing closure, and it is quite remarkable that Beamish & Crawford expressed an interest in saving it. Even though both breweries were competitors, there existed a great respect for each others time-honoured brewing traditions. It is quite ironic that the eventual saviour of Murphy's Brewery, the Dutch brewing group Heineken, have decided to close down Beamish & Crawford. The announcement that Beamish & Crawford is to be closed leaves a bad taste on any Cork stout drinker's palate.

Promoting Fine Arts

The Cork Society for the Promoting of the Fine Arts was established following the Munster Exhibition of 1815. Its organising committee consisted of artists, architects and patrons of the arts. About this time a series of remarkable classical casts, by the famous Venetian sculptor Canova, were commissioned by the pope and presented to King George IV when he was the Prince of Wales. Through the intervention of Lord Listowel of Convamore, the casts were donated to the citizens of Cork and the Society of Fine Arts was entrusted with their safe-keeping. In 1818 the society was located at No. 95 Patrick Street and extended to the side of Falkiner's Lane which was the site of the former Apollo Theatre. The enrolment of subscribers consisted of prominent persons and gentry.

The old theatre received a new lease of life when it was modified to accommodate the precious casts. The pit was boarded over, the gallery rearranged and the statues were exhibited by the society. Unfortunately, the exhibition was short-lived as just ten years later the Cork Society became bankrupt and the Canova casts were seized for non-payment of rent. The society was bailed out by rich patrons and the debt of £500 was paid, the casts were then rehoused in the Royal Cork Institution. The statues of Apollo, Belvedere, Antinous, Mithridates, Maria Louisa, Venus de Medici, Juno, Ariadne, Adonis, Napoleon's mother, a piping fawn, Bacchus, Cicero, Socrates, a cow, a lion and a hundred other fine men, beautiful women, divine gods and goddesses, and remarkable animals were all rescued from a very uncertain fate.

By 1828, the Royal Institution became involved in educating local artists, with the aim of preventing them from travelling abroad to learn their craft. John Bolster, an antiquarian and the British government's official printer in Cork, printed a pamphlet extolling the virtues of using these Canova casts to teach students. He waxed lyrical on the temptations of young artists drawing from live models, where their morals would be sorely tempted. The idea of their young minds exposed to naked flesh at such a tender age could either crack or warp their brains. The Society of Arts was quick to impose censorship on paintings on the grounds of excessive nudity. One of the most celebrated cases was the painting by James Barry, 'Venus Rising from the Sea', which had to be withdrawn due to the morals of the day. Another painting by a Cork artist, Thomas Falvey, depicting a group of boys bathing was also considered indecent and suffered the same fate. Falvey left the city bitterly disappointed and spent two years living a meagre existence on the continent before he returned to Cork to exhibit once more.

In 1858, the matter of art education was being discussed in the *Cork Examiner*, which lamented the fact that the local schools were not receiving a proper grant from the state to encourage art education. The bulk of the money was spent on funding a staff of inspectors to go to the schools to award paper testimonials and copper medals. Two years previously one hundred medals were offered in a competition throughout the schools of Britain and Ireland, with no institution to receive more than five medals. Cork had the distinction of winning three, but it took two years for them to arrive. When they were being awarded it was discovered that the silver medals had been magically transformed into a base copper version. A contemporary account by Richard Sainthill stated that:

> The awkward letters of apology accompanying the medals did nothing for their poor design. The noble figure of Justice leered like a harlot and Genius was recognisable only by indications of poverty.

The life of a budding artist, irrespective of their talent, was fraught with financial difficulties: how could one survive on such a meagre wage? Cork was far away from the capital of the art world in London, so local artists needed a patron to promote their works and artistic ability if they were to be successful. One such artist was Daniel Maclise, whose talents were recognised by the wealthy banker Mr Newenham and the wine merchant Richard Sainthill. But a little good fortune in the shape of Sir Walter Scott's visit to Cork was to catapult him to fame and fortune. Sir Walter Scott had his portrait sketched by this unknown artist at Bolster's bookshop and five hundred lithographs of this were printed and sold immediately. In 1827, he left for London and was helped in his endeavours by the antiquarian Crofton Croker and well-known travel writers Mr and Mrs S.C. Hall.

He quickly established himself as a leading artist in London, became the toast of London society and was a close friend of Charles Dickens. For his painting 'The Spirit of Justice', he was awarded the sum of 250 guineas and commissioned to reproduce it for the palace of Westminster.

Around that time it was lamented that the works of artists were valued chiefly for what they fetched and were for collectors mere objects of speculation and investment. The case of Jonathan Butts springs to mind. This talented painter never reached the dizzy heights of some of his contemporaries. He was recognised as a talented Cork painter and his pupil was Nathaniel Grogan who was well known for his paintings of Cork, but he never achieved the fame or fortune that he deserved. To survive and feed his family he had to painting stage sets for the theatre. He became an alcoholic and ended his days in poverty. But the story of Jonathan Butts was not to end there; almost two hundred and fifty years later, his 'View of Cork' *c.*1760 was auctioned in Cork. This painting had been attributed to his pupil Nathaniel Grogan, but extensive research had proven that Butts was indeed the painter. 'The View of Cork' made a staggering €700,000 at Lyne & Lyne's Cork auction and fortunately thanks to the generosity of a local businessman, it was saved for the city. It now hangs in the Crawford Art Gallery where it can be viewed and appreciated by all of Cork's art lovers.

The *Sirius*

The St George Steam Packet Company was founded by Joseph Robinson Pim in 1821. Its first two vessels were the *St Patrick* and the *St George*. The *St Patrick* had the distinction of becoming the first all-steam vessel to enter St George's Channel and the Atlantic. The first two steamships of the St George Company to trade directly with Cork were the *Lee* and the *Severn*. These ships were built at Wilson's yard in Liverpool in 1825. The *Lee* serviced the Mersey route whilst the *Severn* plied the Bristol route. Competition was to intensify when a group of Cork merchants, headed by Ebenezer Pike, acquired the steamship *Superb*. Fares were cut, brass bands were employed to entertain the passengers and loaves of bread were given free of charge to prospective travellers.

Initially the St George Steam packet company had its head office at Warrens Place but in 1831 its headquarters were relocated to Penrose Quay. A carved stone effigy of St George slaying the dragon was positioned directly over the entrance. By the year 1834 steamship technology had come of age, as ships were carrying London newspapers to Cork on the Bristol run a full thirty hours before the arrival of the Holyhead mail which ran less frequently. In 1837 the steamship *Sirius* was constructed by Menzie & Co. of Leith and the engineering firm of Wingsale & Co. supplied the latest 320 horse power engines. The schooner rigged ship was built at a cost of £27,000. The figurehead was a dog holding a star between its paws, representing the dog star Sirius. The *Sirius* had two masts, a single funnel and it was one hundred and seventy-eight feet long, weighing four hundred and seventeen tons.

Lieutenant Richard Roberts, a native of Passage, was appointed captain in 1838. Roberts was born in 1803 and because of his interest in sailing he enrolled in the British navy at an early age. He quickly rose through the ranks and was promoted to lieutenant because of his success in engaging slave ships off the coast of Africa, notably the capture of *El Almirat* in 1829. By 1830 the British navy had become overstaffed and Roberts left the service on a small pension. He joined the St George Steam Packet Company and became captain of the *Victory*, on the Cork to Bristol route. His opportunity to acquire fortune and fame came when he was commissioned to captain the *Sirius* on its first transatlantic voyage to New York.

Several firms had plans to be the first to cross the Atlantic to New York by employing the latest techniques in steam engineering. The Great Western Railway Company was engaged in building the *Great Western* which was designed by one of the greatest engineers of his day, Isembard Kingdom Brunel. On 19 July 1837, this new ship was launched amid great pomp and ceremony. The hull was towed to the shipyard of Maudslay, Son & Field in London to have her specially developed engines fitted. The *Great Western* was specifically built for the transatlantic crossing and the firm were quite confident that she was the best vessel afloat for the job. But there was not enough time to carry out sea trials, so the *Great Western* was to be tested for the first time on her maiden voyage in the treacherous waters of the Atlantic.

James Beale was the first to decide to try and charter the *Sirius* from the St George Steam Packet Company on behalf of the British & American Steam Navigation Co. This was at a time when the safety aspect of steam navigation was in its infancy and shipwrecks were a common occurrence, even on short haul trips. A long crossing carried with it greater risks and greater possibilities of storm-force conditions. The David v. Goliath battle for the fastest crossing began when the *Sirius* left Passage in Cork on 28 March 1838 and the *Great Western* left London on 7 April 1838. The *Sirius* carried forty passengers and a cargo which included barrels of Beamish & Crawford extra stout. The *Cork Constitution* advertised fares of eighty guineas first class, twenty guineas second class and finally steerage, eight guineas. Paying passengers on the *Sirius* meant profit for the company.

Shortly into her voyage the *Great Western* caught fire, losing valuable time and forfeiting the majority of her fifty passengers who quickly deserted the ship when they pulled into port for repairs. She was to steam to New York with only seven passengers on board. The *Sirius* was packed to capacity, carried four hundred and fifty tons of coal and had a top speed of nine knots. But all was not well as she encountered strong gales and rough seas, and some of the passengers and crew demanded that she turn back. Despite this, Captain Roberts carried on. As the *Sirius* neared New York the supplies of coal ran out and the crew laid their hands on everything that they could burn. The ship's emergency mast, doors and furniture were all thrown into the boiler to keep up a head of steam. On 22 April she steamed into New York Harbour, smoke pouring from her funnel in triumph. Hours later the *Great Western* arrived, with a very dejected Captain Hosken declaring that the *Sirius* had cheated by topping up her coals.

Civic receptions, banquets and lavish parties were the order of the day. The little paddle steamer *Sirius* and Captain Roberts were fêted all over New York. The pioneering age of transatlantic steam crossing had finally come of age and with it the new era of sail giving way to steam.

Tom Green

Tom Green was a well-known Cork character in the mid 1800s. His father was an army tailor and so he travelled a great deal as a child, even as far as the island of Martinique. France was still at war with England when the family returned to Ireland and landed at Cobh. Shortly afterward, Tom's father died. He had the unusual surname of Arthbutnot, and it was said that his mother remarried a gentleman by the name of Green, due to the shortness of his name, which Tom later adopted.

Tom had a vivid imagination and his early voyages as a young boy provided him with ample recollections. He told stories of voyages around the Cape, of dolphins, flying fish, crossing the line of Neptune and stories of mermaids and attacks by sea monsters.

When Tom was young he was a post-boy at McDowell's Imperial Hotel on the South Mall. One evening as he was watering a pair of horses near the channel at Hanover Street, one of the horses slipped and Tom was thrown into the swollen river. The current dragged him under the Southgate Bridge and down river to near Copley's dock at the end of Copley Street. He was rescued by passers-by who threw him a rope to secure under his arms and he was pulled safely ashore.

Another of his duties at McDowell's was to drive condemned criminals to their execution. At that time the

practice was to hang the culprit near the scene of the crime. Once he had to drive three condemned men, a priest and Canty, the hangman, to Twopothouse near Mallow where they were to be executed, one at a time. One day it was a hanging, the next day it could be a wedding or driving a honeymoon couple to Killarney. On one such occasion, Tom stopped to prepare his lunch of goat's milk, bread, Kerry butter and of course a drop of old Cork whiskey. But, Tom had parked too close to the edge of the roadway and down they went, horses coach and all into a steep embankment landing safely in the nearby bog, unhurt. Tom was severely reprimanded by his employer for his carelessness.

As Tom grew older his plump face developed into the

most remarkable set of wrinkles, grooves and hollows that were ever seen, by anyone. He accounted for his mass of wrinkles by saying: 'I fell on a gravel walk when I was a small boy.' He always kept himself well, and even though his boots were old and broken they always were polished and shone like new. He kept his pipe, matches and tobacco in his blue cloth cap, always at the ready.

Tom's one weakness was whiskey, for which he had a particular fondness. At that time a glass of whiskey could be purchased for one penny. Your pennyworth bought you a measure known as a small Darby. Because Tom had no teeth, his mouth could hold the exact measure so he always knew when the publican had supplied the required amount. The historian and antiquarian Robert Day recalled that when he was about to sit down to dinner he would say grace, a short prayer that God would bless the providers and most importantly of all, the consumers. Tom would then put a potato into his toothless mouth and roll it back and forth until it was digested. The contortions on his face were extremely funny and one day he was approached by a well-known firm of brass founders who offered him five shillings for a cast of his face. Tom refused, but if he had accepted his features would have become the best known in the city, appearing on every door knocker in Cork.

Tom lived to the ripe old age of one hundred years, which he attributed to the whiskey he consumed during his lifetime. He was as honest as the days are long; a devout Catholic, although he did once admit with all sincerity that he would steal whiskey from the Pope.

Bibliography

PARLIAMENTARY PAPERS

Municipal Corporations in Ireland. Report on the City of Cork (London 1833)

Returns & Accounts Relating to the Foundling Hospital Cork (London 1854)

The Charter of the Commercial Buildings Company of Cork (Cork 1809)

An Act to Raise a Fund for Defraying the Charge of Commercial Improvements Within the City & Port of Cork (London 1814)

An Act for Building a Bridge over the North Channel of the River Lee (Dublin 1786).

An Act for Establishing an Infirmary in the City of Cork (Dublin 1752)

Report from the Select Committee on the Cork Election Petition (London 1853)

REPORTS

American Commission on Conditions in Ireland Interim Report (Washington D.C. 1921)

American Commission Evidence on Conditions in Ireland (Washington D.C. 1921)

Irish Labour Party. Who Burnt Cork City? (Dublin 1921)

UNPUBLISHED THESIS

Lenihan, Michael, *Some Aspects of Printing and Literature in Cork City, 1750-1900,* Unpublished M.A. thesis UCC (Cork 2002)

BOOKS & JOURNALS

Alexander the Coppersmith, *Remarks upon the Religion, Trade, Government, Police, Customs, Manners, and Maladys, of the City of Cork* (1st edition, Cork 1737)

Bates, W., *The Maclise Portrait Gallery* (London 1883)

Beecher, Sean, *Day by Day. A Miscellany of Cork History* (Cork 1992)

Besnard, Andre, *A Tale of Old Cork* (Cork 1889)

Bielenberg, Andy, *Cork's Industrial Revolution: Development or Decline?* (Cork 1991)

Bolster, Evelyn Sr, *A History of the Diocese of Cork*, 4 vols (1972-1993)

Bolster, John, *The Bye Laws & Charters of Cork* (Cork 1822)

Bolster, John, *Bolster's Quarterly Magazine*, Vol. I (Cork 1826)

Bullingbrooke, Edward, *The Duty and Authority of the Justices of the Peace and Parish Officers for Ireland* (Dublin 1766)

Cambell, Thomas, *A Philosophical Survey of the South of Ireland* (Dublin 1778)

Caulfield, R. (ed.), *The Council Book of the Corporation of the City of Cork* (Guilford 1876)

Caulfield, R. (ed.) (1877), *The register of the parish of the Holy Trinity (Christ Church), Cork, from July 1643, to February 1668, with extracts from the parish books, from 1664 to 1668* (Cork 1877)

Caulfield, R., *Handbook of the Cathedral Church of St. Finbarre Cork* (Cork 1881)

Caulfield, R., *Annals of St. Finbarre's Cathedral Cork* (Cork 1871)

Caulfield, R., *A Lecture on the History of the Bishops of Cork* (Cork 1864)

Census of Ireland, Vol. 11, Province of Munster (Dublin 1882)

Cody, Bryan, *The River Lee. Cork and the Corkonians* (1st edition, Cork 1859)

Coleman. J.C., *Journeys into Muskerry* (Dundalk 1958)

Cooke R.T., *My Home by the Lee* (Cork 1999)

Coppinger, Walter Arthur (ed.), *History of the Copingers or Coppingers of the county of Cork, Ireland, and the counties of Suffolk and Kent, England* (London 1878)

Cork International Exhibition and South of Ireland Souvenir (Cork 1902)

Greater Cork International Exhibition and South of Ireland Souvenir (Cork 1903)

Cork. Its Trade & Commerce (Cork 1919)

Costello, C., *In Quest of an Heir* (Cork 1978)

Croft, C., *The Memoirs of Charles Crofts* (Cork 1829)

Croker, T.C., *Researches in the South of Ireland* (1st edition, London 1824)

Croker, T.C., *The Keen of the South of Ireland* (London 1844)

Croker, T.C., *Fairy Legends and Traditions of the South of Ireland* (London 1862)

Cronin, M., *Country, Class or Craft. The Politicisation of the Skilled Artisan in 19th-Century Cork* (Cork 1994)

D'Alton, I., *Protestant Society and Politics in Cork 1812-1844* (Cork 1980)

Daly, S., *Cork: A City in Crisis* (Cork 1978)

Davis, T., *The Speeches of the Right Honorable John Philpot Curran* (Dublin 1853)

De Latocnaye, J., *Rambles through Ireland* (Cork 1798)

Dunne Sean (ed.) The Cork Anthology (Cork 1993)

Dwyer, Rev. J.A., *The Dominicans of Cork City and County* (Cork. 1896)

Edwards, A., *Cork Remembrancer* (Cork 1792)

Egan, Fr B., *The Friars of Broad Lane Collectors Edition* (Cork 1977)

Fitzgerald, J., *The Cork Rembrancer* (Cork 1783)

Fitzgerald, J., *Echoes of 98* (Cork 1898)

Fitzgerald, J., *Legends, Ballads and Songs of the Lee* (Cork 1913)

Foley, C., *A History of Douglas* (Cork 1981)

Gibson, Rev. C., *The History of the County and City of Cork*, 2 vols (London 1861)

Goldberg, Gerald V., *Jonathan Swift and Contemporary Cork* (Cork 1967)

Guy, F., *Descriptive & Gossiping Guide to the South of Ireland* (Cork 1883)

Hall, S.C., *Ireland: its Scenery, Character and History*, 6 vols (Boston 1911)

Haly, J., *The Monthly Miscellany or Irish Review & Register* (Cork 1796)

Harrison, R., *Cork City Quakers* (Privately published 1991)

Henchion, Richard, *Henchion's Cork Centenary Remembrancer 1887* (Cork 1986)

Hodges, Rev. J., *Cork & County Cork in the Twentieth Century* (Brighton 1911)

Hood, S., *Register of the Parish of Holy Trinity (Christ Church Cork) 1643-1669* (Dublin 1998)

Jenkins, S., *The Cork & Muskerry Light Railway* (Oxford 1992)

Johnson, G., *The Laneways of Medieval Cork* (Cork 2002)

Journal of the Cork Historical and Archaeological Society (Cork 1892-2001)

Lewis, C., *A Topographical Dictionary of Ireland*, 2 vols (London 1837)

McCarthy, J.G., *The History of Cork* (2nd edition, Cork 1869)

McGrath, W., *Some Industrial Railways of Ireland* (Cork 1959)

McGrath, W., *Tram Tracks Through Cork* (Cork 1981)

Maguire, J.F., *The National Exhibition of 1852* (Cork 1853)

Maguire, J.F., *Father Mathew: A Biography* (London 1863)

Munter, R., *The History of the Irish Newspaper 1685-1760* (Cambridge 1967)

Munter, R., *A Dictionary of the Print Trade in Ireland 1550-1775* (New York 1988)

Murphy, J., *Terra Incognita* (London 1873)

North, J.S., *The Waterloo Directory of Irish Newspapers and Periodicals, 1800-1900* (Ontario 1986)

O'Callaghan, G., *Fr. Franciscan Cork* (Cork 1953)

O'Donoghue, F., *Tomás MacCurtain* (Kerry 1958)

O'Drisceoil, D. & O'Drisceoil, D., *The Murphy's Story* (Cork 1997)

O'Flanagan, P. & Buttimer C.G. (eds), *Cork: History & Society* (Dublin 1993)

O'Hegarty, P.S., *A Short Memoir of Terence MacSwiney* (Dublin 1922)

O'Kelly, E., *The Old Private Banks and Bankers of Munster* (Cork 1959)

O'Mahony, S., *The Reliques of Father Prout*, 2 Vols (1st edition, London 1836)

O'Sullivan, W., *The Economic History of Cork* (Cork 1937)

Phelps, W., *Irish Glass. The Age of Exhuberance* (New York 1970)

Pike, J., *Some Account of the Life of Joseph Pike* (London 1837)

Rebel Cork's Fighting Story (1st edition, Kerry 1947)

Robinson, A.C., *Rev. St. Finbarre's Cathedral Cork* (Cork 1897)

Roche, J., *Critical and Miscellaneous Essays* (Cork 1851)

Sainthill, R., *Supplement to Numismatic Crumbs* (Cork 1859)

Sheahan, T., *Articles of Irish Manufacture or Portions of Cork History* (Cork 1833)

Simmington, R.C., *The Civil Survey 1654-56* (Dublin 1942)

Smith, C., *The Antient and Present State of the County and City of Cork* (first edition Dublin 1750)

Smith, C., *The Antient and Present State of the County and City of Cork* (third edition, Cork 1815)

Smith, C., *The Antient and Present State of the County and City of Cork* (fourth edition Cork 1893)

Spolasco, Baron, *The Narrative of the Wreck of the* Killarney (Cork 1838)

Townsend, Rev. H., *A General & Statistical Survey of the County of Cork* (Cork 1815)

Twiss, R., *A Tour in Ireland in 1775* (second edition, Dublin 1776)

Tuckey, F.H., *The Cork Remembrancer. Part 11* (first edition, Cork 1838)

Wall, T., *The Sign of Doctor Hay's Head* (Dublin 1958)

Windele, J., *Historical and Descriptive Notices of the City of Cork and its Vicinity* (1st edition, Cork 1839)

CATALOGUES

Gurr Auctioneers, *Catalogue of the Collection of the Late Robert Day* (Cork 1915)

Lynes & Lynes, *Cork Sale Catalogue,* 24 May 2005 (Cork 2005)

Offical Catalogue, *Greater Cork International Exhibition 1903* (Cork 1903)

(Roche & Keating) *Cork Furniture Stores Catalogue* (Cork 1910)

PAMPHLETS

Landon, H., *Corkiana Compiled from Old Cork Newspapers* (Cork 1905)

Everybody, V., *A Run through the South of Ireland* (Cork 1852)

J.C.P., *A Visit to Henry Ford & Son, Ltd Marina Cork* (Dublin 1927)

Ford & Son, *The First Sixty Years 1917-1977: Ford in Ireland* (Cork 1977)

O'Brien, J.B., *Catholic Middle Classes in Pre Famine Cork* (NUI 1981)

Prospectus for Rebuilding St. Finbarr's Cork, September 26th 1863.

DIRECTORIES AND ALMANACS

Aldwell's *Post Office Directory for the Years 1844-1845* (Cork 1845)

Connor's *Cork Directory* (Cork 1812)

Connor's *Cork Directory* (Cork 1817)

Connor's *Cork Directory* (Cork 1826)

County & City of Cork Post office General Directory, 1842-3 (Australia 1996)

Guy's County & City of Cork Directory for 1875-1876 (Cork 1876)

Haly's Cork Directory for 1795 (Cork 1795)

Lucas, R., *Cork Directory for 1787* (Cork 1787)

Henry & Coughlan's General Directory of Cork (Cork 1867)

Holden's Triennial Directory for 1805, 1806 and 1807. Vol 2. (London 1805)

Nash's Sixpenny Almanac for the Year of Our Lord 1842 (Cork 1842)

Purcell's Commercial Cork Almanac for 1883 (Cork 1883)

Wallace, Rev. C., 'A Brief Directory of the City of Cork, 1758 and 1769-1770', in *The Irish Genealogist*, Vol. I, No 8. (Dublin 1940)

West, W. A., *Directory of Cork, 1809-1810* (Cork 1810)

NEWSPAPERS

Cork Advertiser & Commercial Register

Cork Chronicle

Cork Constitution

Cork Evening Echo

Cork Examiner

Cork Freeholder

Cork Hollybough

Corke Journal

Hibernian Chronicle

The Illustrated London News

The New Cork Evening Post

The Southern Reporter